When You Look Back

RASHMA MEHTA

MA PUBLISHER

Published by MA Publishing
Published in UK
ISBN-13: 978-1-910499-41-2

Cover designed by Mayar Akash
Cover photo by Mayar Akash
Typeset in Times Roman

Dedication

Poems to dedicate to Vishal

You break through, Loyalty, Hold you, You are my hero, Inspiration, You make me feel, Human being, Personality, You are a star, Host, Best friend, You, Storm, Held my hand, What If, There for me, Thank you, Role model, Had my back, Helped me, Eliminate, Under your wing, Approach, Living proof, Heal me, Unlock, Rise above it, Against me, Light me up, Tear me apart, Reach out to me, Lean on me, Count on me, Vent to me, Have your back, Be your rock, Won't let you fall, Rely on me, Always have me, Won't turn you away, Look my way, Hear you call, Turn to me, Never leave your side, Trust in me, Never let you down, Glue you back together, hurt you, in a blink of an eye, Always be in your corner, when you need me, drag you down, won't walk away, free you, knock you down, look for me, in the blink of a light, in the flesh, in a flash, believe in you, care for you, look out for you, loyal to you for life, take you aside and make you smile, I give you, brave face, fake smile, put on an act, shed a teardrop, inseparable for life, be yourself around me, close by, stick by my word, lead you astray. When I'm around you, never question, you shield me, underground, bring you down, dreams. Backstab you, take advantage of you, betray you, hit a brick wall, doubt yourself, you mean the absolute world to me, never change you, Bring out the warrior in you, bring you out of your shell, look up to you, look up to me, admire you, walk all over you, screw you over, bring out the worst in you, bring out the best in you, perfect to me, walk on fire for you, never run a mile, go that extra mile for you, best intentions, best interest at heart.

I would also like to dedicate the poem "Defeat you" to Jayesh Bhatt.

Acknowledgement

I would like to thank Vishal Bhatnagar, Bhupendra M Gandhi and Tim Webb for always believing in me and supporting me through my writing. They have all been great sources of inspiration, helping me to make my dream go further than ever before. In particular I would like to thank Vishal Bhatnagar who continues to be my inspiration.

I would like to thank all the people for their continued support and being a part of my writing journey and helping me in all their special ways every step of the way.

I would like to thank Monique and Elizabeth for proofreading my work when I needed it most, as every writer needs a proof reader; it plays an important part in publication.

Contents

Dedication	3
Acknowledgement	4
Introduction	9
I Give	10
In The Flesh	11
Blame Game	12
Blink Of A Light	13
Protector	14
Walk Away	15
Free	16
Knock Down	17
Loyalty	18
Look	19
Cave In	20
Care	21
Look Out	22
Loyal	23
Heal	24
Rise Above It	25
Power	25
In A Flash	26
Believe In	27
Never Let	28
Crumble	29
Smile	30
Against	31
You Have	32
Keep Close	32
When	33
Every Inch	33
Drag Down	34
Reservations	35
Brave	36
Crossroads	37
Fake	38
Stand Tall	39
An Act	40
Pick Myself	41
Intoxicated	42

Yourself	43
Angel Eyez	44
Unlock	45
Teardrop	46
Spiral	47
Vision	47
Inseparable	48
Worst Enemy	49
Close By	50
Stick By	51
Dreams	52
Family Loyalty	52
Untangle	53
Lead Astray	54
Illusion	55
Around You	56
Defeat	57
Bring You Down	58
So Caught Up	59
Never Question	60
Connection	60
Underground	61
Shield Me	62
Storm	63
Backstab	64
Hold	65
Take Advantage	66
Betray	68
Hit A Brick Wall	70
Break Through	71
Doubt	72
Feel	73
The Absolute World	74
If	75
Never Change	76
Wish	77
Up To You	78
A Star	79
Up To Me	80
Host	81
Your Shell	82
Admire	84

Cling	85
The Warrior	86
Drown	87
Screw	88
Eliminate	89
The Best	90
Let My Voice	91
Perfect	92
Over You	93
The Worst	95
Walk On Fire	97
Errors	98
Never	99
Extra Mile	100
Intentions	101
Interest	103
B F	105
Hero	106
Inspiration	107
Human Being	108
My Hand	109
For Me	110
Imperfections	111
Thank You	112
Fall Out	113
Role Model.	114
My Back	115
Under Your Wing	117
Approach	118
Vision Impairment	119
Living Proof	120
Light	122
Individuality	123
Apart	124
Reach Out	125
Lean On	126
Vent	127
Count	128
Your Back	129
Rock	130
Rely	131
Fall	132

Turn You	133
Personality	134
Always	135
Hear You	136
My Way	137
Trust	138
To Me	139
Your Side	140
Never Let You	141
Glue You Back	142
Hurt You	143
You Helped	144
Blink Of An Eye	145
In Your Corner	146
When You Need	147
Index	148

Introduction

Following on from my first book, the experience and the attention has taken me to another lever. I feel fulfilled, accomplished and satisfied all in one and yet the thought of publishing my next book, that feeling grips me, I want to repeat it. All this energy has put me in a state of constantly wanting to express more, let my thoughts and insights to flow in to my books. I now have realised my writing passion of mine since 2008 and I find myself constantly re – inspired by my life experiences.

I hope my books continue to enlighten my readers whilst also maintaining an element of surprise. I aspire to take my writing to its next level through hard work, perseverance and sheer determination. I would like to thank my family and friends for this, as without their ongoing support I would not be able to continue along my journey.

This book is filled with even more exciting, original material. The direction has slightly changed based on my experiences. Additionally, I have chosen to explore new styles and techniques as a writer, which I hope my readers will enjoy.

I Give

I give you my heart.
I give you my soul.
I give you my honesty.
I give you my strength.
I give you my energy.
I give you my hope.
I give you my loyalty.
I give you my bravery.
I give you my fearless ways of being.
I give you my confidence.
I give you the real me
I give you the true me.
I give you my vision of life.

In The Flesh

When you look back at your fragile past, know I will always appear in the flesh
When you face you your lifelong fears, know I will always appear in the flesh.
When you try and break your lifelong issues that affect you, know I will always appear in the flesh.
When you try and overcome the loneliness you feel, know I will always appear in the flesh.

When you feel down, know I will always appear in the flesh.
If and when you feel broken, know I will always appear in the flesh.
When you feel like you're in a dark place, know I will always appear in the flesh.
When you feel like you're struggling, know I will always appear in the flesh.

When your inner cries take its toll on you, know I will always appear in the flesh.
When you don't feel strong enough, know I will always appear in the flesh.
When you don't feel brave enough, know I will always appear in the flesh.
When you feel low, know I will always appear in the flesh.

When you feel lost in any way, know I will always appear in the flesh.
When you need a shoulder to cry on, know I will always appear in the flesh.
If and when you don't feel good enough, know I will always appear in the flesh.
When you feel like an outsider, know I will always appear in the flesh.

If and when you feel rejected, know I will always appear in the flesh.
When you feel like giving up, know I will always appear in the flesh.
If and when you feel unwanted, know I will always appear in the flesh.
If and when you feel worthless, know I will always appear in the flesh.

When you feel like you are entering an unknown trap, know I will appear in the flesh.
When you feel like you're in denial, know I will always appear in the flesh.
If and when you have nowhere to turn, know I will always appear in the flesh.
If and when you don't feel you have the courage to fight, know I will always appear in the flesh.

If and when you feel insecure, know I will always appear in the flesh.
If and when you feel guilt in any way, know I will always appear in the flesh.
When you need me the most, know I will always appear in the flesh.
When you are not yourself, know I will always appear in the flesh.

When you feel alone, know I will always appear in the flesh.
When you face challenging days, I will walk along side you and know I will always appear in the flesh.
If and when you need to vent, know I will always appear in the flesh.

Blame Game

I took the blame for this toxic environment.
I took the blame for the way I was raised in a toxic environment.
I took the blame for the vengeance I hold within.
I took the blame for the way I was treated.

I took the blame for feeling like a nobody.
I took the blame for the way I turned out.
I took the blame for the protection of those that are close to and beside me.
I took the blame for the rebel I became.

I took the blame for the screw up I was.
I took the blame for feeling like an outsider.
I took the blame for feeling unwanted.
I took the blame for anything and everything that got thrown my way.

I took the blame for the rejection I felt.
I took the blame for the people around me to keep them safe.
I took the blame for the rage I held within.
I took the blame for feeling invisible.
I took the blame for believing things that weren't true.

Blink Of A Light

When you look back at your fragile past, know I will always be there in a blink of light.
When you face you your lifelong fears, know I will always be there in a blink of light.
When you try and break your lifelong issues that affect you, know I will always be there in a blink of light.
When you try and overcome the loneliness you feel, know I will always be there in a blink of light.

When you feel down, know I will always be there in a blink of light.
If and when you feel broken, know I will always be there in a blink of light.
When you feel like you're in a dark place, know I will always be there in a blink of light.
When you feel like you're struggling, know I will always be there in a blink of light.

When your inner cries take its toll on you, know I will always be there in a blink of light.
When you don't feel strong enough, know I will always be there in a blink of light.
When you don't feel brave enough, know I will always be there in a blink of light.
When you feel low, know I will always be there in a blink of light.

When you feel lost in any way, know I will always be there in a blink of light.
When you need a shoulder to cry on, know I will always be there in a blink of light.
If and when you don't feel good enough, know I will always be there in a blink of light.
When you feel like an outsider, know I will always be there in a blink of light.

If and when you feel rejected, know I will always be there in a blink of light.
When you feel like giving up, know I will always be there in a blink of light.
If and when you feel unwanted, know I will always be there in a blink of light.
If and when you feel worthless, know I will always be there in a blink of light.

When you feel like you are entering an unknown trap, know I will always be there in a blink of light.
When you feel like you're in denial, know I will always be there in a blink of light.

If and when you have nowhere to turn, know I will always be there in a blink of light.
If and when you don't feel you have the courage to fight, know I will always be there in a blink of light.
If and when you feel insecure, know I will always be there in a blink of light.
If and when you feel guilt in any way, know I will always be there in a blink of light.
When you need me the most, know I will always be there in a blink of light.
When you are not yourself, know I will always be there in a blink of light.
When you feel alone, know I will always be there in a blink of light.
When you face challenging days, I will walk alongside you and know I will always be there in a blink of light.
If and when you need to vent, know I will always be there in a blink of light.

Protector

Protector of the extension of your heartfelt traumatic past.
Protector of your innocent minds.
Protector of the hurtful reminders that follow you around.
Protector of the devil that tries to corrupt you.

Protector of the pain your soul holds within.
Protector of the unnoticed defence you try and bring out.
Protector of the determination you hold within.
Protector of your inner world.

Protector of your close inner circle.
Protector of your breaking point.
Protector of your heart.
Protector of your weakness.
Protector of the real you.

Walk Away

When you look back at your fragile past, know I won't walk away.
When you face you your lifelong fears, know I won't walk away.
When you try and break your lifelong issues that affect you, know I won't walk away.
When you try and overcome the loneliness you feel, know I won't walk away.

When you feel down, know I won't walk away.
If and when you feel broken, know I won't walk away.
When you feel like you're in a dark place, know I won't walk away.
When you feel like you're struggling, know I won't walk away.

When your inner cries take its toll on you, know I won't walk away.
When you don't feel strong enough, know I won't walk away.
When you don't feel brave enough, know I won't walk away.
When you feel low, know I won't walk away.

When you feel lost in any way, know I won't walk away.
When you need a shoulder to cry on, know I won't walk away.
If and when you don't feel good enough, know I won't walk away.
When you feel like an outsider, know I won't walk way.

If and when you feel rejected, know I won't walk away.
When you feel like giving up, know I won't walk away.
If and when you feel unwanted, know I won't walk away.
If and when you feel worthless, know I won't walk away.

When you feel like you are entering an unknown trap, know I won't walk away.
When you feel like you're in denial, know I won't walk away.
If and when you have nowhere to turn, know I won't walk away.
If and when you don't feel you have the courage to fight, know I won't walk away.

If and when you feel insecure, know I won't walk away.
If and when you feel guilt in any way, know I won't walk away.
When you need me the most, know I won't walk away.
When you are not yourself, know I won't walk away.
When you feel alone, know I won't walk away
When you face challenging days, I will walk alongside you and know I won't walk away.
If and when you need to vent, know I won't walk away.

Free

When you look back at your fragile past, know I will always free you.
When you face you your lifelong fears, know I will always free you.
When you try and break your lifelong issues that affect you, know I will always free you.
When you try and overcome the loneliness you feel, know I will always free you.

When you feel down, know I will always free you.
If and when you feel broken, know I will always free you.
When you feel like you're in a dark place, know I will always free you.
When you feel like you're struggling, know I will always free you.

When your inner cries take its toll on you, know I will always free you.
When you don't feel strong enough, know I will always free you.
When you don't feel brave enough, know I will always free you
When you feel low, know I will always free you.

When you feel lost in any way, know I will always free you.
When you need a shoulder to cry on, know I will always free you.
If and when you don't feel good enough, know I will always free you.
When you feel like an outsider, know I will always free you.

If and when you feel rejected, know I will always free you.
When you feel like giving up, know I will always free you.
If and when you feel unwanted, know I will always free you.
If and when you feel worthless, know I will always free you.

When you feel like you are entering an unknown trap, know I will always free you.
When you feel like you're in denial, know I will always free you.
If and when you have nowhere to turn, know I will always free you.
If and when you don't feel you have the courage to fight, know I will always free you.

If and when you feel insecure, know I will always free you.
If and when you feel guilt in any way, know I will always free you.
When you need me the most, know I will always free you.
When you are not yourself, know I will always free you.
When you feel alone, know I will always free you
When you face challenging days, I will walk alongside you and know I will always free you.
If and when you need to vent, know I will always free you.

Knock Down

When you look back at your fragile past, know I won't let anyone knock you down.
When you face you your lifelong fears, know I won't let anyone knock you down.
When you try and break your lifelong issues that affect you, know I won't let anyone knock you down
When you try and overcome the loneliness you feel, know I won't let anyone knock you down.

When you feel down, know I won't let anyone knock you down.
If and when you feel broken, know I won't let anyone knock you down.
When you feel like you're in a dark place, know I won't let anyone knock you down.
When you feel like you're struggling, know I won't let anyone knock you down.

When your inner cries take its toll on you, know I won't let anyone knock you down.
When you don't feel strong enough, know I won't let anyone knock you down.
When you don't feel brave enough, know I won't let anyone knock you down.
When you feel low, know I won't let anyone knock you down.

When you feel lost in any way, know I won't let anyone knock you down.
When you need a shoulder to cry on, know I won't let anyone knock you down.
If and when you don't feel good enough, know I won't let anyone knock you down.
When you feel like an outsider, know I won't let anyone knock you down.

If and when you feel rejected, know I won't let anyone knock you down.
When you feel like giving up, know I won't let anyone knock you down.
If and when you feel unwanted, know I won't let anyone knock you down.
If and when you feel worthless, know I won't let anyone knock you down.

When you feel like you are entering an unknown trap, know I won't let anyone knock you down.
When you feel like you're in denial, know I won't let anyone knock you down.
If and when you have nowhere to turn, know I won't let anyone knock you down.
If and when you don't feel you have the courage to fight, know I won't let anyone knock you down
If and when you feel insecure, know I won't let anyone knock you down.

If and when you feel guilt in any way, know I won't let anyone knock you down.
When you need me the most, know I won't let anyone knock you down.
When you are not yourself, know I won't let anyone knock you down.
When you feel alone, know I won't let anyone knock you down.
When you face challenging days, I will walk alongside you and know I won't let anyone knock you down.
If and when you need to vent, know I won't let anyone knock you down.

Loyalty

Loyalty to those who accept your past.
Loyalty to those who stick by you though thick and thin.
Loyalty to those who have made an impact on you and your life.
Loyalty to those who stand by you for the person you are.

Loyalty to those who support you for the right reasons.
Loyalty to those who accept you for you.
Loyalty to those who accept you as you are.
Loyalty is not a weakness.
Loyalty is a way to tell who your true friends are.
Loyalty is never facing anything alone.

Look

When you look back at your fragile past, know you can always look for me.
When you face you your lifelong fears, know you can always look for me.
When you try and break your lifelong issues that affect you, know you can always look for me.
When you try and overcome the loneliness you feel, know you can always look for me.

When you feel down, know you can always look for me.
If and when you feel broken, know you can always look for me.
When you feel like you're in a dark place, know you can always look for me.
When you feel like you're struggling, know you can always look for me.

When your inner cries take its toll on you, know you can always look for me.
When you don't feel strong enough, know you can always look for me.
When you don't feel brave enough, know you can always look for me.
When you feel low, know you can always look for me

When you feel lost in any way, know you can always look for me.
When you need a shoulder to cry on, know you can always look for me.
If and when you don't feel good enough, know you can always look for me.
When you feel like an outsider, know you can always look for me.

If and when you feel rejected, know you can always look for me.
When you feel like giving up, know you can always look for me.
If and when you feel unwanted, know you can always look for me.
If and when you feel worthless, know you can always look for me.

When you feel like you are entering an unknown trap, know you can always look for me.
When you feel like you're in denial, know you can always look for me.
If and when you have nowhere to turn, know you can always look for me.
If and when you don't feel you have the courage to fight, know you can always look for me.

If and when you feel insecure, know you can always look for me.
If and when you feel guilt in any way, know you can always look for me.
When you need me the most, know you can always look for me.
When you are not yourself, know you can always look for me.
When you feel alone, know you can always look for me.
When you face challenging days, I will walk alongside you and know you can always look for me.
If and when you need to vent, know you can always look for me.

Cave In

When you look back at your fragile past, know I won't let you cave in.
When you face your lifelong fears, know I won't let you cave in.
When you try and break your lifelong issues that affect you, know I won't let you cave in.
When you try and overcome the loneliness you feel, know I won't let you cave in.

When you feel down, know I won't let you cave in.
If and when you feel broken, know I won't let you cave in.
When you feel like you're in a dark place, know I won't let you cave in.
When you feel like you're struggling, know I won't let you cave in.

When your inner cries take its toll on you, know I won't let you cave in.
When you don't feel strong enough, know I won't let you cave in.
When you don't feel brave enough, know I won't let you cave in.
When you feel low, know I won't let you cave in.

When you feel lost in any way, know I won't let you cave in.
When you need a shoulder to cry on, know I won't let you cave in.
If and when you don't feel good enough, know I won't let you cave in.
When you feel like an outsider, know I won't let you cave in.

If and when you feel rejected, know I won't let you cave in.
When you feel like giving up, know I won't let you cave in.
If and when you feel unwanted, know I won't let you cave in.
If and when you feel worthless, know I won't let you cave in.

When you feel like you are entering an unknown trap, know I won't let you cave in.
When you feel like you're in denial, know I won't let you cave in.
If and when you have nowhere to turn, know I won't let you cave in.
If and when you don't feel you have the courage to fight, know I won't let you cave in.

If and when you feel insecure, know I won't let you cave in.
If and when you feel guilt in any way, know I won't let you cave in.
When you need me the most, know I won't let you cave in.
When you are not yourself, know I won't let you cave in.
When you feel alone, know I won't let you cave in.
When you face challenging days, I will walk alongside you and know I won't let you cave in.
If and when you need to vent, know I won't let you cave in.

Care

When you look back at your fragile past, know I will always care for you.
When you face you your lifelong fears, know I will always care for you.
When you try and break your lifelong issues that affect you, know I will always care for you.
When you try and overcome the loneliness you feel, know I will always care for you.

When you feel down, know I will always care for you.
If and when you feel broken, know I will always care for you.
When you feel like you're in a dark place, know I will always care for you.
When you feel like you're struggling, know I will always care for you.

When your inner cries take its toll on you, know I will always care for you.
When you don't feel strong enough, know I will always care for you.
When you don't feel brave enough, know I will always care for you.
When you feel low, know I will always care for you.

When you feel lost in any way, know I will always care for you.
When you need a shoulder to cry on, know I will always care for you.
If and when you don't feel good enough, know I will always care for you.
When you feel like an outsider, know I will always care for you.

If and when you feel rejected, know I will always care for you.
When you feel like giving up, know I will always care for you.
If and when you feel unwanted, know I will always care for you.
If and when you feel worthless, know I will always care for you.

When you feel like you are entering an unknown trap, know I will always care for you.
When you feel like you're in denial, know I will always care for you.
If and when you have nowhere to turn, know I will always care for you.
If and when you don't feel you have the courage to fight, know I will always care for you.

If and when you feel insecure, know I will always care for you.
If and when you feel guilt in any way, know I will always care for you.
When you need me the most, know I will always care for you.
When you are not yourself, know I will always care for you.
When you feel alone, know I will always care for you.
When you face challenging days, I will walk alongside you and know I will always care for you.
If and when you need to vent, know I will always care for you

Look Out

When you look back at your fragile past, know I will always look out for you.
When you face you your lifelong fears, know I will always look out for you.
When you try and break your lifelong issues that affect you, know I will always look out for you.
When you try and overcome the loneliness you feel, know I will always look out for you.

When you feel down, know I will always look out for you.
If and when you feel broken, know I will always look out for you.
When you feel like you're in a dark place, know I will always look out for you.
When you feel like you're struggling, know I will always look out for you.

When your inner cries take its toll on you, know I will always look out for you.
When you don't feel strong enough, know I will always look out for you.
When you don't feel brave enough, know I will always look out for you.
When you feel low, know I will always look out for you.

When you feel lost in any way, know I will always look out for you.
When you need a shoulder to cry on, know I will always look out for you.
If and when you don't feel good enough, know I will always look out for you.
When you feel like an outsider, know I will always look out for you.

If and when you feel rejected, know I will always look out for you.
When you feel like giving up, know I will always look out for you.
If and when you feel unwanted, know I will always look out for you.
If and when you feel worthless, know I will always look out for you.

When you feel like you are entering an unknown trap, know I will always look out for you.
When you feel like you're in denial, know I will always look out for you.
If and when you have nowhere to turn, know I will always look out for you.
If and when you don't feel you have the courage to fight, know I will always look out for you.

If and when you feel insecure, know I will always look out for you.
If and when you feel guilt in any way, know I will always look out for you.
When you need me the most, know I will always look out for you.
When you are not yourself, know I will always look out for you.
When you feel alone, know I will always look out for you.
When you face challenging days, I will walk alongside you and know I will always look out for you.
If and when you need to vent, know I will always look out for you.

Loyal

When you look back at your fragile past, know I will always be loyal to you for life.
When you face you your lifelong fears, know I will always be loyal to you for life.
When you try and break your lifelong issues that affect you, know I will always be loyal to you for life.
When you try and overcome the loneliness you feel, know I will always be loyal to you for life.

When you feel down, know I will always be loyal to you for life.
If and when you feel broken, know I will always be loyal to you for life.
When you feel like you're in a dark place, know I will always be loyal to you for life.
When you feel like you're struggling, know I will always be loyal to you for life.

When your inner cries take its toll on you, know I will always be loyal to you for life.
When you don't feel strong enough, know I will always be loyal to you for life.
When you don't feel brave enough, know I will always be loyal to you for life.
When you feel low, know I will always be loyal to you for life.

When you feel lost in any way, know I will always be loyal to you for life.
When you need a shoulder to cry on, know I will always be loyal to you for life.
If and when you don't feel good enough, know I will always be loyal to you for life.
When you feel like an outsider, know I will always be loyal to you for life.

If and when you feel rejected, know I will always be loyal to you for life.
When you feel like giving up, know I will always be loyal to you for life.
If and when you feel unwanted, know I will always be loyal to you for life.
If and when you feel worthless, know I will always be loyal to you for life.

When you feel like you are entering an unknown trap, know I will always be loyal to you for life.
When you feel like you're in denial, know I will always be loyal to you for life.
If and when you have nowhere to turn, know I will always be loyal to you for life.
If and when you don't feel you have the courage to fight, know I will always be loyal to you for life
If and when you feel insecure, know I will always be loyal to you for life.

If and when you feel guilt in any way, know I will always be loyal to you for life.
When you need me the most, know I will always be loyal to you for life.
When you are not yourself, know I will always be loyal to you for life.
When you feel alone, know I will always be loyal to you for life.
When you face challenging days, I will walk alongside you and know I will always be loyal to you for life.
If and when you need to vent, know I will always be loyal to you for life.

Heal

You heal my fragile past.
You heal my fragile heart.
You heal my heartache.
You heal my pain.

You heal my troubles that follow me.
You heal my lifelong traumas.
You heal my disbelief.
You heal my denial.

You heal my hurt
You heal the way I am.
You heal the energetic demons.
You heal my loneliness.
You heal my need for revenge.
You heal my need for vengeance.
You heal my need to succeed.
You heal the need to fix wonky ne.

Rise Above It

As I look back at my fragile past you help me rise above it.
As my lifelong fears terrorise me to no end you help me rise above it.
As an ugly side of me comes firing out at me you help me rise above it.
As my state of mind comes back to trigger something in me you help me rise above it.

As my rage tries to take hold of me you pull me out and help me rise above it.
As the anger in me comes to light you help me rise above it.
With my hour of need lurking around you help me rise above it.
As my battles make a u turn from the back of my mind you help me rise above the beasts and beat them.

As my loneliness takes its toll on me you come crashing in and help me rise above it.
As my mood changes from happy to dark you help me rise above it.
As I feel down you lift my mood and help me rise above it.
As I feel broken you patch me back together and help me rise above it.
As I feel lost you bring me back from a world that isn't for me and you help me rise above it.
When my walls crack wide open you come racing in and help me rise above it.

Power

You got the power to determine if ur past will be a constant loss.
You got the power to come face to face with things that antagonise you and solve it.
You got the power to not give the wrong people ammunition over you.
You got the power to not let things escalate in any situation.
You got the power to escape the pain you feel.
You got the power to deal with difficulties in life that try and overtake us.
You got the power to figure out who you wanna be.
You got the power to let people that love you into ur life and know they will stay with you step by step.
You got the power to deflate the doubts in ur head.
You got the power to turn the atmosphere of the environment ur in around.

In A Flash

When you look back at your fragile past, know I will always appear in a flash.
When you face you your lifelong fears, know I will always appear in a flash.
When you try and break your lifelong issues that affect you, know I will always appear in a flash.
When you try and overcome the loneliness you feel, know I will always appear in a flash.

When you feel down, know I will always appear in a flash.
If and when you feel broken, know I will always appear in a flash.
When you feel like you're in a dark place, know I will always appear in a flash.
When you feel like you're struggling, know I will always appear in a flash.

When your inner cries take its toll on you, know I will always appear in a flash.
When you don't feel strong enough, know I will always appear in a flash.
When you don't feel brave enough, know I will always appear in a flash.
When you feel low, know I will always appear in a flash.

When you feel lost in any way, know I will always appear in a flash.
When you need a shoulder to cry on, know I will always appear in a flash.
If and when you don't feel good enough, know I will always appear in a flash.
When you feel like an outsider, know I will always appear in a flash.

If and when you feel rejected, know I will always appear in a flash.
When you feel like giving up, know I will always appear in a flash.
If and when you feel unwanted, know I will always appear in a flash.
If and when you feel worthless, know I will always appear in a flash.

When you feel like you are entering an unknown trap, know I will appear in a flash.
When you feel like you're in denial, know I will always appear in a flash.
If and when you have nowhere to turn, know I will always appear in a flash.
If and when you don't feel you have the courage to fight, know I will always appear in a flash.

If and when you feel insecure, know I will always appear in a flash.
If and when you feel guilt in any way, know I will always appear in a flash.
When you need me the most, know I will always appear in a flash.
When you are not yourself, know I will always appear in a flash
When you feel alone, know I will always appear in a flash
When you face challenging days, I will walk alongside you and know I will always appear in a flash
If and when you need to vent, know I will always appear in a flash

Believe In

When you look back at your fragile past, know I will always believe in you.
When you face you your lifelong fears, know I will always believe in you.
When you try and break your lifelong issues that affect you, know I will always believe in you.
When you try and overcome the loneliness you feel, know I will always believe in you.

When you feel down, know I will always believe in me.
If and when you feel broken, know I will always believe in you.
When you feel like you're in a dark place, know I will always believe in you.
When you feel like you're struggling, know I will always believe in you.

When your inner cries take its toll on you, know I will always believe in you.
When you don't feel strong enough, know I will always believe in you.
When you don't feel brave enough, know I will always believe in you.
When you feel low, know I will always believe in you.

When you feel lost in any way, know I will always believe in you.
When you need a shoulder to cry on, know I will always believe in you.
If and when you don't feel good enough, know I will always believe in you.
When you feel like an outsider, know I will always believe in you.

If and when you feel rejected, know I will always believe in you.
When you feel like giving up, know I will always believe in you.
If and when you feel unwanted, know I will always believe in you.
If and when you feel worthless, know I will always believe in you.

When you feel like you are entering an unknown trap, know I will always believe in you.
When you feel like you're in denial, know I will always believe in you.
If and when you have nowhere to turn, know I will always believe in you.
If and when you don't feel you have the courage to fight, know I will always believe in you.

If and when you feel insecure, know I will always believe in you.
If and when you feel guilt in any way, know I will always believe in you.
When you need me the most, know I will always believe in you.
When you are not yourself, know I will always believe in you.
When you feel alone, know I will always believe in you.
When you face challenging days, I will walk alongside you and know I will always believe in you.
If and when you need to vent, know I will always believe in you.

Never Let

When you look back at your fragile past, know I will never let you face anything alone.
When you face you your lifelong fears, know I will never let you face anything alone.
When you try and break your lifelong issues that affect you, know I will never let you face anything alone.
When you try and overcome the loneliness you feel, know I will never let you face anything alone.

When you feel down, know I will never let you face anything alone.
If and when you feel broken, know I will never let you face anything alone.
When you feel like you're in a dark place, know I will never let you face anything alone.
When you feel like you're struggling, know I will never let you face anything alone.

When your inner cries take its toll on you, know I will never let you face anything alone.
When you don't feel strong enough, know I will never let you face anything alone.
When you don't feel brave enough, know I will never let you face anything alone.
When you feel low, know I will never let you face anything alone.

When you feel lost in any way, know I will never let you face anything alone.
When you need a shoulder to cry on, know I will never let you face anything alone.
If and when you don't feel good enough, know I will never let you face anything alone.
When you feel like an outsider, know I will never let you face anything alone.

If and when you feel rejected, know I will never let you face anything alone.
When you feel like giving up, know I will never let you face anything alone.
If and when you feel unwanted, know I will never let you face anything alone.
If and when you feel worthless, know I will never let you face anything alone.

When you feel like you are entering an unknown trap, know I will never let you face anything alone.
When you feel like you're in denial, know I will never let you face anything alone.

If and when you have nowhere to turn, know I will never let you face anything alone
If and when you don't feel you have the courage to fight, know I will never let you face anything alone.
If and when you feel insecure, know I will never let you face anything alone.
If and when you feel guilt in any way, know I will never let you face anything alone.
When you need me the most, know I will never let you face anything alone.
When you are not yourself, know I will never let you face anything alone.
When you feel alone, know I will never let you face anything alone.
When you face challenging days, I will walk alongside you and know I will never let you face anything alone.
If and when you need to vent, know I will never let you face anything alone.

Crumble

Don't let your past crumble to tiny pieces.
Don't let your fears dictate the way it crumbles.
Don't let your pain be the reason it crumbles.
Don't let your own strength force your own hand to crumble.

Don't let your voice be shattered when it crumbles.
Don't let emptiness crumble to the floor.
Don't let emotional strain crumble.
Don't let your determination crumble.

Don't let your demons tackle you to crumble.
Don't let your true self crumble
Don't let the real you crumble.
Don't let the pressure of things around you crumble.
Don't let hope crumble.
Don't let your darkest way crumble.
Don't let your lowest point crumble.
Don't let the tiger in you crumble.

Smile

When you look back at your fragile past, know I will always take you aside and make you smile.
When you face you your lifelong fears, know I will always take you aside and make you smile.
When you try and break your lifelong issues that affect you, know I will always take you aside and make you smile.
When you try and overcome the loneliness you feel, know I will always take you aside and make you smile.

When you feel down, know I will always take you aside and make you smile.
If and when you feel broken, know I will always take you aside and make you smile.
When you feel like you're in a dark place, know I will always take you aside and make you smile
When you feel like you're struggling, know I will always take you aside and make you smile.

When your inner cries take its toll on you, know I will always take you aside and make you smile.
When you don't feel strong enough, know I will always take you aside and make you smile
When you don't feel brave enough, know I will always take you aside and make you smile.
When you feel low, know I will always take you aside and make you smile.

When you feel lost in any way, know I will always take you aside and make you smile.
When you need a shoulder to cry on, know I will always take you aside and make you smile.
If and when you don't feel good enough, know I will always take you aside and make you smile.
When you feel like an outsider, know I will always take you aside and make you smile.

If and when you feel rejected, know I will always take you aside and make you smile.
When you feel like giving up, know I will always take you aside and make you smile.
If and when you feel unwanted, know I will always take you aside and make you smile

If and when you feel worthless, know I will always take you aside and make you smile.

When you feel like you are entering an unknown trap, know I will always take you aside and make you smile.
When you feel like you're in denial, know I will always take you aside and make you smile.
If and when you have nowhere to turn, know I will always take you aside and make you smile.
If and when you don't feel you have the courage to fight, know I will always take you aside and make you smile.
If and when you feel insecure, know I will always take you aside and make you smile.
If and when you feel guilt in any way, know I will always take you aside and make you smile.
When you need me the most, know I will always take you aside and make you smile.
When you are not yourself, know I will always take you aside and make you smile.
When you feel alone, know I will always take you aside and make you smile.
When you face challenging days, I will walk alongside you and know I will always take you aside and make you smile.

If and when you need to vent, know I will always take you aside and make you smile.

Against

You never hold my past against me
You never hold my lifelong fears that terrorise me to no end against me.
You never hold my fragile state against me.
You never hold my hurt against me.

You never hold the fact that I am not perfect against me.
You never hold my pain against me.
You never hold me accountable for what life throws my way.
You never hold the fact that I am different in my own way against me.
You never hold the fact that I can bring out the true me against me.
You never judge the person I am meant to be.

You Have

You have always believed in me.
You have always supported me in everything I've done.
You have always seen the best in me no matter what.
You have always been there for me through the hectic stuff.

You have been my rock.
You have raised my spirits.
You have picked me up when I've fallen to the ground.
You have always stood by me.

I can be me when I'm around you.
I never have to hide who I am from you.
When I feel lost, you always find me and bring me back to reality.
You take me as I am.

We are inseparable.
You are loyal to me.
You understand me like no one else does.
You are true to me in no uncertain way.
You show me the best way to be.

Keep Close

Keep the past close so you can learn from it.
Keep the fears close to learn the way you tackle them.
Keep your insecurities close to learn the truth about what led you to them.
Keep troubles close to learn how to overcome situations that occur.
Keep being you and the best you can be.
Keep fighting to be heard.
Stand your ground and overachieve the things that you want.

When

When I Came off the rails, I tried to get back on track but something was holding me down.
When I came across a solution, I always get knocked however I always get back and leap forward.
When my heart turns dark you shine a light that shows me a way out
When I become reckless you see another side of me.

When I have doubts you always keep me on the straight and narrow.
When I feel alone I know I'm not as I have people around me that care about me and will walk alongside me when I least expect it.
When I break no matter how hard or bad I know I have a flood of people around me.
When battle I face is worth it as it shows that things are worth standing my ground over.

Every Inch

Every inch of my past face it with all ur energy you have.
Every inch of your fear show you can beat the beast.
Every inch of the darkest hour you try and stop from appearing in front of you.
Every inch of struggling ways that show the deep down corner of you.

Every inch of doubt is just a very close call to over think that you will not be in doubtful thoughts.
Every inch is a true battle with experience that you are someone that don't run from battles and you face them head on.
Every inch of the true you that show who you really wanna be as a person.
Every inch of the real world that shows it can be cruel in a way no one sees coming.
Every inch of the real you is not allowing you to be you.
Be who you are and not a fake show that you are original.

Drag Down

When you look back at your fragile past, know I will never let anyone drag you down.
When you face you your lifelong fears, know I will never let anyone drag you down.
When you try and break your lifelong issues that affect you, know I will never let anyone drag you down.
When you try and overcome the loneliness you feel, know I will never let anyone drag you down.

When you feel down, know I will never let anyone drag you down.
If and when you feel broken, know I will never let anyone drag you down.
When you feel like you're in a dark place, know I will never let anyone drag you down.
When you feel like you're struggling, know I will never let anyone drag you down.

When your inner cries take its toll on you, know I will never let anyone drag you down.
When you don't feel strong enough, know I will never let anyone drag you down.
When you don't feel brave enough, know I will never let anyone drag you down.
When you feel low, know I will never let anyone drag you down.

When you feel lost in any way, know I will never let anyone drag you down.
When you need a shoulder to cry on, know I will never let anyone drag you down.
If and when you don't feel good enough, know I will never let anyone drag you down.
When you feel like an outsider, know I will never let anyone drag you down.

If and when you feel rejected, know I will never let anyone drag you down.
When you feel like giving up, know I will never let anyone drag you down.
If and when you feel unwanted, know I will never let anyone drag you down.
If and when you feel worthless, know I will never let anyone drag you down.

When you feel like you are entering an unknown trap, know I will never let anyone drag you down.
When you feel like you're in denial, know I will never let anyone drag you down.

If and when you have nowhere to turn, know I will never let anyone drag you down.
If and when you don’t feel you have the courage to fight, know I will never let anyone drag you down.
If and when you feel insecure, know I will never let anyone drag you down.
If and when you feel guilt in any way, know I will never let anyone drag you down.
When you need me the most, know I will never let anyone drag you down.
When you are not yourself, know I will never let anyone drag you down.
When you feel alone, know I will never let anyone drag you down.
When you face challenging days, I will walk alongside you and know I will never let anyone drag you down.
If and when you need to vent, know I will never let anyone drag you down.

Reservations

Reservations of my past won’t stop me.
Reservations of my fears won’t stop me confronting them.
Reservations are not a way to trap me.
Reservations of my opportunities won’t stand in my way.

Reservations won’t leave me considering my options.
Reservations won’t drag me down.
Reservations of my failed attempts won’t drop me to the ground.
Reservations of the missing pieces won’t determine my outlook on life.

Reservations of this cold winter won’t stop me achieving what I want.
Reservations of my reality won’t try and avoid me.
Reservations of putting on a brave face in front of the most closest people I care about won't stop me doing just that.
Reservations of how strong I can be is undeniable.
Reservations won’t stop the people that are close to me and by my side from being there when I need them and this will show who I have and who I don’t.

Brave

When you look back at your fragile past, know you don't always have to put on a brave face in front of me.
When you face you your lifelong fears, know you don't always have to put on a brave face in front of me.
When you try and break your lifelong issues that affect you, know you don't always have to put on a brave face in front of me.
When you try and overcome the loneliness you feel, know you don't always have to put on a brave face in front of me.

When you feel down, know you don't always have to put on a brave face in front of me.
If and when you feel broken, know you don't always have to put on a brave face in front of me.
When you feel like you're in a dark place, know you don't always have to put on a brave face in front of me.
When you feel like you're struggling, know you don't always have to put on a brave face in front of me.

When your inner cries take its toll on you, know you don't always have to put on a brave face in front of me
When you don't feel strong enough, know you don't always have to put on a brave face in front of me.
When you don't feel brave enough, know you don't always have to put on a brave face in front of me.
When you feel low, know you don't always have to put on a brave face in front of me.

When you feel lost in any way, know you don't always have to put on a brave face in front of me.
When you need a shoulder to cry on, know you don't always have to put on a brave face in front of me.
If and when you don't feel good enough, know you don't always have to put on a brave face in front of me.
When you feel like an outsider, know you don't always have to put on a brave face in front of me.

If and when you feel rejected, know you don't always have to put on a brave face in front of me.
When you feel like giving up, know you don't always have to put on a brave face in front of me.

If and when you feel unwanted, know you don't always have to put on a brave face in front of me.
If and when you feel worthless, know you don't always have to put on a brave face in front of me.
When you feel like you are entering an unknown trap, know you don't always have to put on a brave face in front of me.
When you feel like you're in denial, know you don't always have to put on a brave face in front of me.
If and when you have nowhere to turn, know you don't always have put on a brave face in front of me.
If and when you don't feel you have the courage to fight, know you don't always have to put on a brave face in front of me.
If and when you feel insecure, know you don't always have to put on a brave face in front of me.
If and when you feel guilt in any way, know you don't always have to put on a brave face in front of me.
When you need me the most, know you don't always have to put on a brave face in front of me.
When you are not yourself, know you don't always have to put on a brave face in front of me.
When you feel alone, know you don't always have to put on a brave face in front of me.
When you face challenging days, know you don't always have to put on a brave face in front of me.
If and when you need to vent, know you don't always have to put on a brave face in front of me.

Crossroads

Crossroads appear to block your past.
Crossroads appear to turn that terrorising look on ur face into hope.
Crossroads appear to help chase ur troubles away before they take over ur life.
Crossroads appear to help you with ur echoing voices.

Crossroads appear to be a revolution.
Crossroads appear to help you stay afloat.
Crossroads appear to help you survive the cruel way of the world outside.
Crossroads appear to show you that you are unique.
Crossroads appear to help you realise the battles you face can be vanished from ur life.

Fake

When you look back at your fragile past, know you don't always have to fake a smile around me.
When you face you your lifelong fears, know you don't always have to fake a smile around me.
When you try and break your lifelong issues that affect you, know you don't always have to fake a smile around me.
When you try and overcome the loneliness you feel, know you don't always have to fake a smile around me.
When you feel down, know you don't always have to fake a smile around me.
If and when you feel broken, know you don't always have to fake a smile around me.
When you feel like you're in a dark place, know you don't always have to fake a smile around me.
When you feel like you're struggling, know you don't always have to fake a smile around me.

When your inner cries take its toll on you, know you don't always have to fake a smile around me.
When you don't feel strong enough, know you don't always have to fake a smile around me.
When you don't feel brave enough, know you don't always have to fake a smile around me.
When you feel low, know you don't always have to fake a smile around me.

When you feel lost in any way, know you don't always have to fake a smile around me.
When you need a shoulder to cry on, know you don't always have to fake a smile around me.
If and when you don't feel good enough, know you don't always have to fake a smile around me.
When you feel like an outsider, know you don't always have to fake a smile around me.

If and when you feel rejected, know you don't always have to fake a smile around me.
When you feel like giving up, know you don't always have to fake a smile around me.
If and when you feel unwanted, know you don't always have to fake a smile around me.

If and when you feel worthless, know you don't always have to fake a smile around me.

When you feel like you are entering an unknown trap, know you don't always have to fake a smile around me.
When you feel like you're in denial, know you don't always have to fake a smile around me.
If and when you have nowhere to turn, know you don't always have to fake a smile around me.
If and when you don't feel you have the courage to fight, know you don't always have to fake a smile around me.
If and when you feel insecure, know you don't always have to fake a smile around me.
If and when you feel guilt in any way, know you don't always have to fake a smile around me.
When you need me the most, know you don't always have to fake a smile around me.
When you are not yourself, know you don't always have to fake a smile around me.
When you feel alone, know you don't always have to fake a smile around me.
When you face challenging days, I will walk alongside you and know you don't always have to fake a smile around me.
If and when you need to vent, know you don't always have to fake a smile around me.

Stand Tall

Don't let your past define you stand tall.
Don't let your fears determine you stand tall.
Don't let trouble chase you stand tall.
Don't let confidence knock you sideways stand tall.
Don't doubt your expectations stand tall.
Don't matter how hard you try keep going and stand tall.
Don't let gravity drop you
u to the ground stand tall

An Act

When you look back at your fragile past, know you don't always have to put on an act around me.
When you face you your lifelong fears, know you don't always have to put on an act around me.
When you try and break your lifelong issues that affect you, know you don't always have to put on an act around me.
When you try and overcome the loneliness you feel, know you don't always have to put on an act around me.

When you feel down, know you don't always have to put on an act around me.
If and when you feel broken, know you don't always have to put on an act around me.
When you feel like you're in a dark place, know you don't always have to put on an act around me.
When you feel like you're struggling, know you don't always have to put on an act around me.

When your inner cries take its toll on you, know you don't always have to put on an act around me.
When you don't feel strong enough, know you don't always have to put on an act around me.
When you don't feel brave enough, know you don't always have to put on an act around me.
When you feel low, know you don't always have to put on an act around me.

When you feel lost in any way, know you don't always have to put on an act around me.
When you need a shoulder to cry on, know you don't always have to put on an act around me.
If and when you don't feel good enough, know you don't always have to put on an act around me.
When you feel like an outsider, know you don't always have to put on an act around me.

If and when you feel rejected, know you don't always have to put on an act around me.
When you feel like giving up, know you don't always have to put on an act around me.
If and when you feel unwanted, know you don't always have to put on an act around me.

If and when you feel worthless, know you don't always have to put on an act around me.

When you feel like you are entering an unknown trap, know you don't always have to put on an act around me.
When you feel like you're in denial, know you don't always have to put on an act around me.
If and when you have nowhere to turn, know you don't always have to put on an act around me.
If and when you don't feel you have the courage to fight, know you don't always have to put on an act around me.
If and when you feel insecure, know you don't always have to put on an act around me.
If and when you feel guilt in any way, know you don't always have to put on an act around me.
When you need me the most, know you don't always have to put on an act around me.
When you are not yourself, know you don't always have to put on an act around me.
When you feel alone, know you don't always have to put on an act around me.
When you face challenging days, I will walk alongside you and know you don't always have to put on an act around me.
If and when you need to vent, know you don't always have to put on an act around me.

Pick Myself

I pick myself back up from my horrific past.
I pick myself back up from my traumatic journey of life.
I pick myself back up from my fragile heartache.
I pick myself back up from all the pain I had.
I pick myself back up from the hurt I go through.
I pick myself back up from failure that comes my way and I keep going to make those around me proud.
I pick myself back up from when something tries to break me.
I pick myself back up from the emotional baggage I had.

Intoxicated

When ur past become intoxicated.
When ur fears become intoxicated.
When ur troubles become intoxicated.
When ur inner cries become intoxicated.

When ur inner voice become intoxicated.
When ur terrified demons become intoxicated.
When ur enemy become intoxicated.
When ur pain become intoxicated.

When ur darkest moments become intoxicated.
When ur emotional strain become intoxicated.
When ur emotional baggage become intoxicated.
When ur nightmares become intoxicated.

When ur bad memories become intoxicated.
When ur unbearable secrets become intoxicated.
When the non-existent from ur life become intoxicated.
When the words some people say to you become intoxicated.

Let what people who are not important to you or ur life and what they think go over ur head and keep the close people you care about and have in ur life close and let them in.

Yourself

When you look back at your fragile past, know you can always be yourself around me.
When you face you your lifelong fears, know you can always be yourself around me.
When you try and break your lifelong issues that affect you, know you can always be yourself around me.
When you try and overcome the loneliness you feel, know you can always be yourself around me.

When you feel down, know you can always be yourself around me.
If and when you feel broken, know you can always be yourself around me.
When you feel like you're in a dark place, know you can always be yourself around me.
When you feel like you're struggling, know you can always be yourself around me.

When your inner cries take its toll on you, know you can always be yourself around me.
When you don't feel strong enough, know you can always be yourself around me.
When you don't feel brave enough, know you can always be yourself around me.
When you feel low, know you can always be yourself around me.

When you feel lost in any way, know you can always be yourself around me.
When you need a shoulder to cry on, know you can always be yourself around me.
If and when you don't feel good enough, know you can always be yourself around me.
When you feel like an outsider, know you can always be yourself around me.

If and when you feel rejected, know you can always be yourself around me.
When you feel like giving up, know you can always be yourself around me.
If and when you feel unwanted, know you can always be yourself around me.
If and when you feel worthless, know you can always be yourself around me
When you feel like you are entering an unknown trap, know you can always be yourself around me.
When you feel like you're in denial, know you can always be yourself around me.
If and when you have nowhere to turn, know you can always be yourself around me.

If and when you don't feel you have the courage to fight, know you can always be yourself around me.
If and when you feel insecure, know you can always be yourself around me.
If and when you feel guilt in any way, know you can always be yourself around me.
When you need me the most, know you can always be yourself around me.
When you are not yourself, know you can always be yourself around me.
When you feel alone, know you can always be yourself around me.
When you face challenging days, I will walk alongside you and know you can always be yourself around me.
If and when you need to vent, know you can always be yourself around me.

Angel Eyez

Angel eyez shine on you when you least expect it.
Angel eyez look down on your reality and help you rally around.
When no one around you understands you angel eyez accepts you for you.
When no one believes your problems angel eyez will help you solve them.

When you feel you Can't face reality angel eyez will keep you on the straight and narrow.
When you feel low angel eyez will guide you through the unnecessary burden on your shoulders.
Angel eyez will always find a way in to your horrific past.
Angel eyez will always hold you close and help you take steps forward.
Angel eyez will always be beside you.
Angel eyez will never judge the choices and decisions you make.

Unlock

I unlock my fragile past as I look into it with you beside me.
I unlock my lifelong fears that terrorise me to no end with you beside me.
I unlock my pain with you beside me.
I unlock m reality as I stumble upon it with you beside me.

I unlock my deepest secrets which don't have a hold over me with you beside me.
I unlock my uniqueness of me with you beside me.
I unlock my rage as everything gets the better of me.
I unlock my thoughts in my head with you beside me.

I unlock my loneliness as it tries to take hold of me with you beside me.
I unlock my hatred to try and release it with you beside me.
I unlock my heart to let those who care about me in with you beside me.
I unlock my tears that stream down my face with you beside me.
I unlock ur shoulder as you let me wipe my tears on you with you beside me.

I unlock my reasons behind my emotion for only you to see and know with you beside me.
I unlock my dilemmas that creep up on me without notice with you beside me.
I unlock the way I strain myself with you beside me.
I unlock my rejection and release it into the open with you beside me.
I unlock my guilt that overwhelms me with you beside me.
I unlock a way for you to always make me smile any way you can.
I unlock the hateful words I hear and I release them into the open air with you beside me.

Teardrop

When you look back at your fragile past, know you can shed a teardrop on me.
When you face you your lifelong fears, know you can shed a teardrop on me.
When you try and break your lifelong issues that affect you, know you can shed a teardrop on me.
When you try and overcome the loneliness you feel, know you can shed a teardrop on me.

When you feel down, know you can shed a teardrop on me.
If and when you feel broken, know you can shed a teardrop on me.
When you feel like you're in a dark place, know you can shed a teardrop on me.
When you feel like you're struggling, know you can shed a teardrop on me.

When your inner cries take its toll on you, know you can shed a teardrop on me.
When you don't feel strong enough, know you can shed a teardrop on me.
When you don't feel brave enough, know you can shed a teardrop on me.
When you feel low, know you can shed a teardrop on me.

When you feel lost in any way, know you can shed a teardrop on me.
When you need a shoulder to cry on, know you can shed a teardrop on me.
If and when you don't feel good enough, know you can shed a teardrop on me.
When you feel like an outsider, know you can shed a teardrop on me.

If and when you feel rejected, know you can shed a teardrop on me.
When you feel like giving up, know you can shed a teardrop on me.
If and when you feel unwanted, know you can shed a teardrop on me.
If and when you feel worthless, know you can shed a teardrop on me.

When you feel like you are entering an unknown trap, know you can shed a teardrop on me.
When you feel like you're in denial, know you can shed a teardrop on me.
If and when you have nowhere to turn, know you can shed a teardrop on me.
If and when you don't feel you have the courage to fight, know you can shed a teardrop on me.
If and when you feel insecure, know you can shed a teardrop on me.
If and when you feel guilt in any way, know you can shed a teardrop on me.
When you need me the most, know you can shed a teardrop on me.
When you are not yourself, know you can shed a teardrop on me.
When you feel alone, know you can shed a teardrop on me.
When you face challenging days, I will walk alongside you and know you can shed a teardrop on me.
If and when you need to vent, know you can shed a teardrop on me.

Spiral

Things that spiral out of control you know you can get it sorted with the right encouragement.
Things that conspire without your knowledge is easily turned with the right mindset.
When things get difficult you come across a way to deal with it when you turn to the people beside you or in your life.
When things turn ugly you can escape reality for a while by turning your attention to the people beside you.
When things turn against you, you don't let it defeat you, you turn to the people who will stick by you.
Don't let those things that don't want you to succeed define you in any way.

Vision

Vision of ur past.
Vision of ur terrorising fears.
Vision of ur territory that you hold close.
Vision of ur own strength.
Vision of ur own enemy.
Vision of ur chemistry.
Vision of ur nightmare.
Vision of ur negativity.
Vision of ur outlook on life.
Vision of ur struggling ways.
Vision of ur doubts.
Vision of ur positivity.
Vision of ur fearless ways.
Vision of ur possible reality.
Vision of ur success.
Vision of ur future which is in ur own very hands.
Vision of ur destiny.
Vision of ur own strong mind.
Vision of ur own path.
Vision of ur own decisions.
Don't let anything stand in ur way be who you wanna be.

Inseparable

When you look back at your fragile past, know we will always be inseparable for life.
When you face you your lifelong fears, know we will always be inseparable for life.
When you try and break your lifelong issues that affect you, know we will always be inseparable for life.
When you try and overcome the loneliness you feel, know we will always be inseparable for life.

When you feel down, know we will always be inseparable for life.
If and when you feel broken, know we will always be inseparable for life.
When you feel like you're in a dark place, know we will always be inseparable for life.
When you feel like you're struggling, know we will always be inseparable for life.

When your inner cries take its toll on you, know we will always be inseparable for life.
When you don't feel strong enough, know we will always be inseparable for life
When you don't feel brave enough, know we will always be inseparable for life.
When you feel low, know we will always be inseparable for life.

When you feel lost in any way, know we will always be inseparable for life.
When you need a shoulder to cry on, know we will always be inseparable for life.
If and when you don't feel good enough, know we will always be inseparable for life.
When you feel like an outsider, know we will always be inseparable for life.

If and when you feel rejected, know we will always be inseparable for life.
When you feel like giving up, know we will always be inseparable for life.
If and when you feel unwanted, know we will always be inseparable for life.
If and when you feel worthless, know we will always be inseparable for life.

When you feel like you are entering an unknown trap, know we will always be inseparable for life.
When you feel like you're in denial, know we will always be inseparable for life.
If and when you have nowhere to turn, know we will always be inseparable for life.

If and when you don't feel you have the courage to fight, know we will be inseparable for life.
If and when you feel insecure, know we will always be inseparable for life.
If and when you feel guilt in any way, know we will always be inseparable for life.
When you need me the most, know we will always be inseparable for life.
When you are not yourself, know we will always be inseparable for life.
When you feel alone, know we will always be inseparable for life.
When you face challenging days, I will walk alongside you and know we will always be inseparable for life.
If and when you need to vent, know we will always be inseparable for life.

Worst Enemy

Don't let your past be your own worst enemy.
Don't let your fear torture you when it becomes your own worst enemy.
Don't let denial become your own worst enemy.
Don't let your darkness path become your own worst enemy.
Don't let your emotional strain become your own worst enemy.
Don't let my silence be your own worst enemy.
Don't let negativity become your own worst enemy.
Don't let strength overpower you and become your own worst enemy.

Close By

When you look back at your fragile past, know I will always be close by.
When you face you your lifelong fears, know I will always be close by.
When you try and break your lifelong issues that affect you, know I will always be close by.
When you try and overcome the loneliness you feel, know I will always be close by.

When you feel down, know I will always be close by.
If and when you feel broken, know I will always be close by.
When you feel like you're in a dark place, know I will always be close by.
When you feel like you're struggling, know I will always be close by.

When your inner cries take its toll on you, know I will always be close by.
When you don't feel strong enough, know I will always be close by.
When you don't feel brave enough, know I will always be close by.
When you feel low, know I will always be close by.

When you feel lost in any way, know I will always be close by.
When you need a shoulder to cry on, know I will always be close by.
If and when you don't feel good enough, know I will always be close by.
When you feel like an outsider, know I will always be close by.

If and when you feel rejected, know I will always be close by.
When you feel like giving up, know I will always be close by.
If and when you feel unwanted, know I will always be close by.
If and when you feel worthless, know I will always be close by.

When you feel like you are entering an unknown trap, know I will always be close by.
When you feel like you're in denial, know I will always be close by.
If and when you have nowhere to turn, know I will always be close by.
If and when you don't feel you have the courage to fight, know I will always be close by.
If and when you feel insecure, know I will always be close by.
If and when you feel guilt in any way, know I will always be close by.
When you need me the most, know I will always be close by.
When you are not yourself, know I will always be close by.
When you feel alone, know I will always be close by.
When you face challenging days, I will walk alongside you and know I will always be close by.
If and when you need to vent, know I will always be close by.

Stick By

When you look back at your fragile past, know I will always stick by my word.
When you face you your lifelong fears, know I will always stick by my word.
When you try and break your lifelong issues that affect you, know I will always stick by my word.
When you try and overcome the loneliness you feel, know I will always stick by my word.

When you feel down, know I will always stick by my word.
If and when you feel broken, know I will always stick by my word.
When you feel like you're in a dark place, know I will always stick by my word
When you feel like you're struggling, know I will always stick by my word.

When your inner cries take its toll on you, know I will always stick by my word.
When you don't feel strong enough, know I will always stick by my word.
When you don't feel brave enough, know I will always stick by my word.
When you feel low, know I will always stick by my word.

When you feel lost in any way, know I will always stick by my word.
When you need a shoulder to cry on, know I will always stick by my word.
If and when you don't feel good enough, know I will always stick by my word.
When you feel like an outsider, know I will always stick by my word.

If and when you feel rejected, know I will always stick by my word.
When you feel like giving up, know I will always stick by my word.
If and when you feel unwanted, know I will always stick by my word.
If and when you feel worthless, know I will always stick by my word.

When you feel like you are entering an unknown trap, know I will always stick by my word.
When you feel like you're in denial, know I will always stick by my word.
If and when you have nowhere to turn, know I will always stick by my word.
If and when you don't feel you have the courage to fight, know I will always stick by my word.
If and when you feel insecure, know I will always stick by my word.
If and when you feel guilt in any way, know I will always stick by my word.
When you need me the most, know I will always stick by my word.
When you are not yourself, know I will always stick by my word.
When you feel alone, know I will always stick by my word.
When you face challenging days, I will walk alongside you and know I will always stick by my word.
If and when you need to vent, know I will always stick by my word.

Dreams

Never let your fragile past determine your dream.
Never let your fears that terrorise you to no end determine your dream.
Never let the darkness of your inner world sway you from achieving your dreams.
Never let the cruelty of this world stop you achieving what you want in life.

If you want to leave a mark on this world go chase the dream of a lifetime.
When you work hard it will always pay off in the end result.
Never let anyone stop you believing in yourself and the dream you so badly want to achieve.
Surround yourself with good vibes and the dream will fall into place.
Be proud of your achievements and keep the dream alive in so many ways.
Never doubt your abilities and capabilities and chase the dram and prove that you are original.
Make your dreams a reality and prove them who didn't believe in you wrong.

Family Loyalty

Family loyalty is never simple.
Family loyalty is draining.
Family loyalty is the way to destroy someone they love if they can't believe in them.
Family loyalty can hurt.

Family loyalty can leave you feeling alone.
Family loyalty can leave you feeling betrayed.
Family loyalty can leave you feeling uneasy.
Family loyalty can leave you further from when you were once close.

Family loyalty can leave you feeling unwanted.
Family loyalty can leave you feeling rejected.
Family loyalty can leave you feeling broken more than ever.
Family loyalty can leave you feeling distant form them.

Untangle

When you look back at your fragile past, know I will always untangle you.
When you face you your lifelong fears, know I will always untangle you.
When you try and break your lifelong issues that affect you, know I will always untangle you.
When you try and overcome the loneliness you feel, know I will always untangle you.

When you feel down, know I will always untangle you.
If and when you feel broken, know I will always untangle you.
When you feel like you're in a dark place, know I will always untangle you.
When you feel like you're struggling, know I will always untangle you.

When your inner cries take its toll on you, know I will always untangle you.
When you don't feel strong enough, know I will always untangle you.
When you don't feel brave enough, know I will always untangle you.
When you feel low, know I will always untangle you.

When you feel lost in any way, know I will always untangle you.
When you need a shoulder to cry on, know I will always untangle you.
If and when you don't feel good enough, know I will always untangle you.
When you feel like an outsider, know I will always untangle you.

If and when you feel rejected, know I will always untangle you.
When you feel like giving up, know I will always untangle you.
If and when you feel unwanted, know I will always untangle you.
If and when you feel worthless, know I will always untangle you.
When you feel like you are entering an unknown trap, know I will untangle you.
When you feel like you're in denial, know I will always untangle you.
If and when you have nowhere to turn, know I will always untangle you.
If and when you don't feel you have the courage to fight, know I will always untangle you.
If and when you feel insecure, know I will always untangle you.
If and when you feel guilt in any way, know I will always untangle you.
When you need me the most, know I will always untangle you.
When you are not yourself, know I will always untangle you.
When you feel alone, know I will always untangle you.
When you face challenging days, I will walk alongside you and know I will always untangle you.
If and when you need to vent, know I will always untangle you.

Lead Astray

When you look back at your fragile past, know I will always make sure no one leads you astray.
When you face you your lifelong fears, know I will always make sure no one leads you astray.
When you try and break your lifelong issues that affect you, know I will always make sure no one leads you astray.
When you try and overcome the loneliness you feel, know I will always make sure no one leads you astray.

When you feel down, know I will always make sure no one leads you astray.
If and when you feel broken, know I will always make sure no one leads you astray.
When you feel like you're in a dark place, know I will always make sure no one leads you astray.
When you feel like you're struggling, know I will always make sure no one leads you astray.

When your inner cries take its toll on you, know I will always make sure no one leads you astray.
When you don't feel strong enough, know I will always make sure no one leads you astray.
When you don't feel brave enough, know I will always make sure no one leads you astray.
When you feel low, know I will always make sure none leads you astray.

When you feel lost in any way, know I will always make sure no one leads you astray.
When you need a shoulder to cry on, know I will always make sure no one leads you astray.
If and when you don't feel good enough, know I will always make sure no one leads you astray.
When you feel like an outsider, know I will always make sure no one leads you astray.

If and when you feel rejected, know I will always make sure no one leads you astray.
When you feel like giving up, know I will always make sure no one leads you astray.
If and when you feel unwanted, know I will always make sure no one leads you astray.

If and when you feel worthless, know I will always make sure no one leads you astray.

When you feel like you are entering an unknown trap, know I will always make sure no one leads you astray.
When you feel like you're in denial, know I will always make sure no one leads you astray.
If and when you have nowhere to turn, know I will always make sure no one leads you astray.
If and when you don't feel you have the courage to fight, know I will always make sure no one leads you astray.
If and when you feel insecure, know I will always make sure no one leads you astray.
If and when you feel guilt in any way, know I will always make sure no one leads you astray.
When you need me the most, know I will always make sure no one leads you astray.
When you are not yourself, know I will always make sure no one leads you astray.
When you feel alone, know I will always make sure no one leads you astray.
When you face challenging days, I will walk alongside you and know I will always make sure no one leads you astray.
If and when you need to vent, know I will always make sure no one leads you astray.

Illusion

Fear is an illusion.
Reality is a false sense of how to be.
False hope is an illusion.
False predictions is an illusion.

False sense of choice is an illusion.
False sense of doubt is an illusion.
False sense of determination is an illusion.
False sense of insecurity is an illusion.

Around You

When I'm around you I feel blessed.
When I'm around you I feel like I don't have to hide the true me.
When I'm around you, you make me feel alive in any way you can.
When I'm around you I know I can be open.

When I'm around you I feel like I can be me.
When I'm around you I know I'll never be alone.
When I'm around you I find I am happiest of all.
When I'm around you, you make me feel like I'm good enough.

When I'm around you I know you have the best intentions for me.
When I'm around you I know I feel valued.
When I'm around you I know I wouldn't trade you for anything.
When I'm around you I feel inspired.

When I'm around you I feel brave to achieve everything I ever wanted
When I'm around you I know you won't let me down in any way.
When I'm around you I feel have someone to turn to when I need to.
When I'm around you nothing ever gets me down.

When I'm around you I know you will always be there for me when I need you the most.
When I'm around you, you make me smile in any way you can.
When I'm around you I don't have to hide my emotions.
When I'm around you I know I will never walk alone.

Defeat

I won't let your fragile past defeat you in any way.
I won't let your fears that terrorise you to no end defeat you in any way.
I won't let your troubles that follow you defeat you in any way.
I won't let you doubt your awesome abilities in any way.

I won't let demons over take you in any way.
Whatever life throws ur way I won't let you face it alone and we will always face it together.
I won't let anything ever come between us
When you need me, I will always come to your aid.

When we are together you always make me feel free from my reality.
When we are together you always make me feel like an incredible sister.
Without you I don't know what I'd do.
You keep me going any way possible.

When I am apart from you there isn't a day, minute, hour, second, I don't think about you.
I wish I could be around and with you 24/7.
When we are together I never wanna leave your side.
When we are together you make me feel like I don't have a care in the world.

You mean everything to me and I will always be a part of you no matter what.
When we are together you make me feel happier then when I'm not around you.
When I cry, I cry because it indicates that I miss you when we are thousands of miles apart and I hate it.
When I'm around you, you make me feel good enough in myself.

When we are together you make me the proudest sister ever.
When we are together you make me feel braver then I could ever be.
When we are together you make me feel stronger than ever.
I know if I didn't have you in my life I wouldn't have got as far as I have.
When we are together you make my life so much better in so many ways.
When we are together you always have the best intentions for me.
You are perfect to me in every way.
I wouldn't trade you for the world.

Bring You Down

When you look back at your fragile past, know I will always make sure no one brings you down.
When you face your lifelong fears, know I will always make sure no one brings you down.
When you try and break your lifelong issues that affect you, know I will always make sure no one brings you down.
When you try and overcame the loneliness you feel, know I will always make sure no one brings you down.

When you feel down, know I will always make sure no one brings you down.
If and when you feel broken, know I will always make sure no one brings you down.
When you feel like you're in a dark place, know I will always make sure no one brings you down.
When you feel like you're struggling, know I will always make sure no one brings you down.

When your inner cries take its toll on you, know I will always make sure no one brings you down.
When you don't feel strong enough, know I will always make sure no one brings you down.
When you don't feel brave enough, know I will always make sure no one brings you down.
When you feel low, know I will always make sure no one brings you down.

When you feel lost in any way, know I will always make sure no one brings you down.
When you need a shoulder to cry on, know I will always make sure no one brings you down.
If and when you don't feel good enough, know I will always make sure no one brings you down.
When you feel like an outsider, know I will always make sure no one brings you down.

If and when you feel rejected, know I will always make sure no one brings you down.
When you feel like giving up, know I will always make sure no one brings you down.
If and when you feel unwanted, know I will always make sure no one brings you down.

If and when you feel worthless, know I will always make sure no one brings you down.
When you feel like your entering an unknown trap, know I will always make sure no one brings you down.
When you feel like you're in denial, know I will always make sure no one brings you down.
If and when you have nowhere to turn, know I will always make sure no one brings you down.
If and when you feel you don't have the courage to fight, know I will always make sure no one brings you down.
If and when you feel insecure, know I will always make sure no one brings you down.
If and when you feel guilt in any way, know I will always make sure no one brings you down.
When you need me the most, know I will always make sure no one brings you down.
When you are not yourself, know I will always make sure no one brings you down.

When you feel alone, know I will always make sure no one brings you down.
When you face challenging days, I will walk alongside you and know I will always make sure no one brings you down.
If and when you need to vent, know I will always make sure no one brings you down.

So Caught Up

I'm so caught up in the past I've created.
I'm so caught up in fearless fears of my world that I try and conquer.
I'm so caught up in the hardship of this cruel world.
I'm so caught up in my own uniqueness.
I'm so caught up in making my own memories in any way I possibly can.
I'm so caught up in making people around me proud.
I'm so caught up in my own struggling ways to make them disappear.
I'm so caught up in my own doubts.
I'm so caught up in making an impact o the people around me.
I'm so caught up in making a difference.
I'm so caught up in making memorable moments with the people around me.

Never Question

Never question your fragile past as your past is only a reminder.
Never question how you reach your dreams in your own unique way.
Never question the way your life runs as life itself takes you on a journey of a lifetime.
Never question the value of yourself.

Never question how strong you can be.
Never question how brave you are.
Never question your abilities and capabilities within yourself.
Never question the outcome of your life as it will lead you down the right path in the end.

Never question the battles you face as they show how far you have come to get where you are.
Never question that someone no matter where they are will always be there to give you the hope, strength and courage you need.
Never question the determination you have to focus on the good things that come your way.

Connection

Connection is possible.
Connection is a turning point.
Connection is being true to those around you.
Connection allows you to face reality with the support of those around you.

Connection allows you to find yourself.
Connection allows you to see what is around the corner.
Connection allows you to believe in yourself and those around you.
Connection allows you to do what is best for you with the encouragement of those around you.

Connection allows you to forget the hurt you feel and turn to those around you.
When you feeling low connection allows you to be able to turn to those around you.
Connection allows you to see the people who will stick by you.
Connection allows you to see the people who love you for you.

Underground

when you look back at your fragile past, know I will always take you underground.
When you face your lifelong fears, know I will always take you underground.
When you try and break your lifelong issues that affect you, know I will always take you underground.
When you try and overcame the loneliness you feel, know I will always take you underground.

When you feel down, know I will always take you underground.
If and when you feel broken, know I will always take you underground.
When you feel like you're in a dark place, know I will always take you underground.
When you feel like you're struggling, know I will always take you underground.

When your inner cries take its toll on you, know I will always take you underground.
When you don't feel strong enough, know I will always take you underground.
When you don't feel brave enough, know I will always take you underground.
When you feel low, know I will always take you underground.

When you feel lost in any way, know I will always take you underground.
When you need a shoulder to cry on, know I will always take you underground.
If and when you don't feel good enough, know I will always take you underground.
When you feel like an outsider, know I will always take you underground.

If and when you feel rejected, know I will always take you underground.
When you feel like giving up, know I will always take you underground.
If and when you feel unwanted, know I will always take you underground.
If and when you feel worthless, know I will always take you underground.

When you feel like your entering an unknown trap, know I will always take you underground.
When you feel like you're in denial, know I will always take you underground.
If and when you have nowhere to turn, know I will always take you underground.
If and when you feel you don't have the courage to fight, know I will always take you underground.

If and when you feel insecure, know I will always take you underground.

If and when you feel guilt in any way, know I will always take you underground.
When you need me the most, know I will always take you underground.
When you are not yourself, know I will always take you underground.
When you feel alone, know I will always take you underground.
When you face challenging days, I will walk alongside you and know I will always take you underground.
If and when you need to vent, know I will always take you underground.

Shield Me

You shield me from my fragile past.
You shield me from the fears that terrorise me to no end.
You shield me from the pain I feel.
You shield me from the coldest of this dark winter.

You shield me from the hurt I feel.
You shield me from the cruelty of this world.
You shield me from the hatred I feel within.
You shield me from the true intentions of this world we live in.
You shield me from breaking my heart into a thousand pieces.

You shied me from the toughest of times.
You shield me from my darkest of days.
You shield me from feeling rejected.
You shield me from feeling worthless.

You shield me from feeling like a nobody.
You shield me from the betrayal I feel from others.
You shield me from the false hope I sometimes feel.
You shield me from my demons that try and scare me in to not facing them.

Storm

Ur an amazing storm.
Ur an incredible storm.
Ur an inspirational storm.
Ur a fabulous storm.

Ur an excellent storm.
Ur an extraordinary storm.
Ur a tremendous storm.
Ur a fighting spirit storm.

Ur a force of nature storm.
Ur an outstand storm.
Ur a carefree storm.
Ur a free spirit storm.

Ur a loyal storm.
Ur a great storm.
Ur a passionate storm.
Ur a mega storm.

Ur a magical storm.
Ur a determined storm.
Ur a magnificent storm.
Ur a star storm.

Ur a true storm.
Ur a worthy storm.
Ur a firestorm.
Ur a genuine storm.
Ur a rare storm.
Ur a strong storm.

Backstab

When you look back at your fragile past, know I will never let anyone backstab you.
When you face you your lifelong fears, know I will never let anyone backstab you.
When you try and break your lifelong issues that affect you, know I will never let anyone backstab you.
When you try and overcome the loneliness you feel, know I will never let anyone backstab you.
When you feel down, know I will never let anyone backstab you.
If and when you feel broken, know I will never let anyone backstab you.
When you feel like you're in a dark place, know I will never let anyone backstab you.
When you feel like you're struggling, know I will never let anyone backstab you.

When your inner cries take its toll on you, know I will never let anyone backstab you.
When you don't feel strong enough, know I will never let anyone backstab you.
When you don't feel brave enough, know I will never let anyone backstab you.
When you feel low, know I will never let anyone backstab you.

When you feel lost in any way, know I will never let anyone backstab you.
When you need a shoulder to cry on, know I will never let anyone backstab you.
If and when you don't feel good enough, know I will never let anyone backstab you.
When you feel like an outsider, know I will never let anyone backstab you.

If and when you feel rejected, know I will never let anyone backstab you.
When you feel like giving up, know I will never let anyone backstab you.
If and when you feel unwanted, know I will never let anyone backstab you.
If and when you feel worthless, know I will never let anyone backstab you.

When you feel like you are entering an unknown trap, know I will never let anyone backstab you.
When you feel like you're in denial, know I will never let anyone backstab you.
If and when you have nowhere to turn, know I will never let anyone backstab you.
If and when you don't feel you have the courage to fight, know I will never let anyone backstab you.

If and when you feel insecure, know I will never let anyone backstab you.
If and when you feel guilt in any way, know I will never let anyone backstab you.
When you need me the most, know I will never let anyone backstab you.
When you are not yourself, know I will never let anyone backstab you.
When you feel alone, know I will never let anyone backstab you.
When you face challenging days, I will walk alongside you and know I will never let anyone backstab you.
If and when you need to vent, know I will never let anyone backstab you.

Hold

I'm going to hold you as you face ur fragile past.
I'm going to hold you as you face ur energetic demons.
I'm going to hold you as you face the tough things that are thrown ur way.
I'm going to hold you as you face the nightmares that occur.

I'm going to hold you if you fall apart.
I'm going to hold you if something tries to break you.
I'm going to hold you as you take one step at a time towards ur dreams.
I'm going to be there to hold you as you face ur reality.

I'm going to hold you as you chase the uncertainty.
I'm going to hold you as you face backlashes of ur wrong doing.
I'm going to hold you as ur inner cries take control.
I'm going to hold you if and when you become sad.

I'm going to hold you during ur darkest moments.
I'm going to hold you at ur lowest point.
I'm going to hold you at ur weakest point.
I'm going to hold you at ur bravest point.
I'm going to keep hold of you when ur scared.
I'm going to hold you at ur strongest.
I'm going to hold you as you take on challenging days.
I'm going to hold you as you face ur toughest choices.

Take Advantage

When you look back at your fragile past, know I will never let anyone take advantage of you.
When you face you your lifelong fears, know I will never let anyone take advantage of you.
When you try and break your lifelong issues that affect you, know I will never let anyone take advantage of you.
When you try and overcome the loneliness you feel, know I will never let anyone take advantage of you.

When you feel down, know I will never let anyone take advantage of you.
If and when you feel broken, know I will never let anyone take advantage of you.
When you feel like you're in a dark place, know I will never let anyone take advantage of you.
When you feel like you're struggling, know I will never let anyone take advantage of you.

When your inner cries take its toll on you, know I will never let anyone take advantage of you.
When you don't feel strong enough, know I will never let anyone take advantage of you.
When you don't feel brave enough, know I will never let anyone take advantage of you.
When you feel low, know I will never let anyone take advantage of you.

When you feel lost in any way, know I will never let anyone take advantage of you.
When you need a shoulder to cry on, know I will never let anyone take advantage of you.
If and when you don't feel good enough, know I will never let anyone take advantage of you.
When you feel like an outsider, know I will never let anyone take advantage of you.

If and when you feel rejected, know I will never let anyone take advantage of you.
When you feel like giving up, know I will never let anyone take advantage of you.
If and when you feel unwanted, know I will never let anyone take advantage of you.

If and when you feel worthless, know I will never let anyone take advantage of you.

When you feel like you are entering an unknown trap, know I will never let anyone take advantage of you.
When you feel like you're in denial, know I will never let anyone take advantage of you.
If and when you have nowhere to turn, know I will never let anyone take advantage of you.
If and when you don't feel you have the courage to fight, know I will never let anyone take advantage of you.
If and when you feel insecure, know I will never let anyone take advantage of you.
If and when you feel guilt in any way, know I will never let anyone take advantage of you.
When you need me the most, know I will never let anyone take advantage of you.
When you are not yourself, know I will never let anyone take advantage of you.
When you feel alone, know I will never let anyone take advantage of you.
When you face challenging days, I will walk alongside you and know I will never let anyone take advantage of you
If and when you need to vent, know I will never let anyone take advantage of you.

Betray

When you look back at your fragile past, know I will never let anyone betray you in any way.
When you face you your lifelong fears, know I will never let anyone betray you in any way.
When you try and break your lifelong issues that affect you, know I will never let anyone betray you in any way.
When you try and overcome the loneliness you feel, know I will never let anyone betray you in any way.

When you feel down, know I will never let anyone betray you in way.
If and when you feel broken, know I will never let anyone betray you in any way.
When you feel like you're in a dark place, know I will never let anyone betray you in any way.
When you feel like you're struggling, know I will never let anyone betray you in any way.

When your inner cries take its toll on you, know I will never let anyone betray you in any way.
When you don't feel strong enough, know I will never let anyone betray you in any way.
When you don't feel brave enough, know I will never let anyone betray you in any way.
When you feel low, know I will never let anyone betray you in any way.

When you feel lost in any way, know I will never let anyone betray you in any way.
When you need a shoulder to cry on, know I will never let anyone betray you in any way.
If and when you don't feel good enough, know I will never let anyone betray you in any way
When you feel like an outsider, know I will never let anyone betray you in any way.

If and when you feel rejected, know I will never let anyone betray you in any way.
When you feel like giving up, know I will never let anyone betray you.
If and when you feel unwanted, know I will never let anyone betray you in any way.

If and when you feel worthless, know I will never let anyone betray you in any way.

When you feel like you are entering an unknown trap, know I will never let anyone betray you in any way.
When you feel like you're in denial, know I will never let anyone betray you in any way.
If and when you have nowhere to turn, know I will never let anyone betray you in any way.
If and when you don't feel you have the courage to fight, know I will never let anyone betray you in any way.
If and when you feel insecure, know I will never let anyone betray you in any way.
If and when you feel guilt in any way, know I will never let anyone betray you in any way.
When you need me the most, know I will never let anyone betray you in any way.
When you are not yourself, know I will never let anyone betray you in any way.
When you feel alone, know I will never let anyone betray you in any way.
When you face challenging days, I will walk alongside you and know I will never let anyone betray you in any way.
If and when you need to vent, know I will never let anyone betray you in any way.

Hit A Brick Wall

When you look back at your fragile past, know I will never let you hit a brick wall.
When you face you your lifelong fears, know I will never let you hit a brick wall.
When you try and break your lifelong issues that affect you, know I will never let you hit a brick wall.
When you try and overcome the loneliness you feel, know I will never let you hit a brick wall.

When you feel down, know I will never let you hit a brick wall.
If and when you feel broken, know I will never let you hit a brick wall.
When you feel like you're in a dark place, know I will never let you hit a brick wall.
When you feel like you're struggling, know I will never let you hit a brick wall.

When your inner cries take its toll on you, know I will never let you hit a brick wall.
When you don't feel strong enough, know I will never let you hit a brick wall.
When you don't feel brave enough, know I will never let you hit a brick wall.
When you feel low, know I will never let you hit a brick wall.

When you feel lost in any way, know I will never let you hit a brick wall.
When you need a shoulder to cry on, know I will never let you hit a brick wall.
If and when you don't feel good enough, know I will never let you hit a brick wall.
When you feel like an outsider, know I will never let you hit a brick wall.

If and when you feel rejected, know I will never let you hit a brick wall.
When you feel like giving up, know I will never let you hit a brick wall.
If and when you feel unwanted, know I will never let you hit a brick wall.
If and when you feel worthless, know I will never let you hit a brick wall.

When you feel like you are entering an unknown trap, know I will never let you hit a brick wall.
When you feel like you're in denial, know I will never let you hit a brick wall.
If and when you have nowhere to turn, know I will never let you hit a brick wall.
If and when you don't feel you have the courage to fight, know I will never let you hit a brick wall.
If and when you feel insecure, know I will never let you hit a brick wall.
If and when you feel guilt in any way, know I will never let you hit a brick wall.
When you need me the most, know I will never let you hit a brick wall.

When you are not yourself, know I will never let you hit a brick wall.
When you feel alone, know I will never let you hit a brick wall.
When you face challenging days, I will walk alongside you and know I will never let you hit a brick wall.
If and when you need to vent, know I will never let you hit a brick wall.

Break Through

You break though my fragile past.
You break though my never-ending pain
You break though my over turning reality
You break though my heart to find the unknown answers

You break though my weakness to see me at my lowest and help me beat it
You know when to break me away from suffering silently
You know when to understand me
You know when I am in denial

You know when I need to escape from my reality
You know when I need to be held together as you are there
You know when I will crack and break
You know when I cry you wipe away my tears that fall

You know when I fall you pick me back up in a way only know how
You know when I am in a dark place or sad you always know how to make my day
You give me hope
You give me strength

You know when I start to question myself
You love me for me and never want me to change for anyone
You are always there for me when no one is

Doubt

When you look back at your fragile past, know I will never let you doubt yourself.
When you face you your lifelong fears, know I will never let you doubt yourself.
When you try and break your lifelong issues that affect you, know I will never let you doubt yourself.
When you try and overcome the loneliness you feel, know I will never let you doubt yourself.

When you feel down, know I will never let you doubt yourself.
If and when you feel broken, know I will never let you doubt yourself.
When you feel like you're in a dark place, know I will never let you doubt yourself.
When you feel like you're struggling, know I will never let you doubt yourself.

When your inner cries take its toll on you, know I will never let you doubt yourself.
When you don't feel strong enough, know I will never let you doubt yourself.
When you don't feel brave enough, know I will never let you doubt yourself.
When you feel low, know I will never let you doubt yourself.

When you feel lost in any way, know I will never let you doubt yourself.
When you need a shoulder to cry on, know I will never let you doubt yourself.
If and when you don't feel good enough, know I will never let you doubt yourself.
When you feel like an outsider, know I will never let you doubt yourself.

If and when you feel rejected, know I will never let you doubt yourself.
When you feel like giving up, know I will never let you doubt yourself.
If and when you feel unwanted, know I will never let you doubt yourself.
If and when you feel worthless, know I will never let you doubt yourself.

When you feel like you are entering an unknown trap, know I will never let you doubt yourself.
When you feel like you're in denial, know I will never let you doubt yourself.
If and when you have nowhere to turn, know I will never let you doubt yourself.
If and when you don't feel you have the courage to fight, know I will never let you doubt yourself.
If and when you feel insecure, know I will never let you doubt yourself.
If and when you feel guilt in any way, know I will never let you doubt yourself.
When you need me the most, know I will never let you doubt yourself.

When you are not yourself, know I will never let you doubt yourself.
When you feel alone, know I will never let you doubt yourself.
When you face challenging days, I will walk alongside you and know I will never let you doubt yourself.
If and when you need to vent, know I will never let you doubt yourself.

Feel

You make me feel alive.
You make sure I am never feeling frighten.
You make me feel I am a somebody.
You make me feel good enough.

You make me want to just go that extra mile for you.
You make me feel like I am worth it.
You never let me walk alone.
You make the true me come out.

You make me smile like no other can.
You make me believe in myself.
You make sure nobody else can hurt me.
You make sure nobody can harm me.

You make sure nobody betrays me.
You make sure I don't face my worst.
You have seen me thrive.
You have seen me sad.

You make sure I don't give up.
You make sure I don't give in.
You make me feel like I can be me.
You make me feel like I don't have to hide the real me from you.

You make me feel like I can do anything.
You bring out the best in me.
You make sure I am never alone.
You always stand by me no matter what.
You make me feel less scared.
You and me have a special bond.
We are inseparable.

The Absolute World

When you look back at your fragile past, know you mean the absolute world to me.
When you face you your lifelong fears, know you mean the absolute world to me.
When you try and break your lifelong issues that affect you, know you mean the absolute world to me.
When you try and overcome the loneliness you feel, know you mean the absolute world to me.

When you feel down, know you mean the absolute world to me.
If and when you feel broken, know you mean the absolute world to me.
When you feel like you're in a dark place, know you mean the absolute world to me.
When you feel like you're struggling, know you mean the absolute word to me.

When your inner cries take its toll on you, know you mean the absolute world to me.
When you don't feel strong enough, know you mean the absolute world to me.
When you don't feel brave enough, know you mean the absolute world to me.
When you feel low, know you mean the absolute world to me.

When you feel lost in any way, know you mean the absolute world to me.
When you need a shoulder to cry on, know you mean the absolute world to me.
If and when you don't feel good enough, know you mean the absolute world to me.
When you feel like an outsider, know you mean the absolute world to me.

If and when you feel rejected, know you mean the absolute world to me.
When you feel like giving up, know you mean the absolute world to me.
If and when you feel unwanted, know you mean the absolute world to me.
If and when you feel worthless, know you mean the absolute world to me.

When you feel like you are entering an unknown trap, know you mean the absolute world to me.
When you feel like you're in denial, know you mean the absolute world to me.
If and when you have nowhere to turn, know you mean the absolute world to me.
If and when you don't feel you have the courage to fight, know you mean the absolute world to me.

If and when you feel insecure, know you mean the absolute world to me.

If and when you feel guilt in any way, know you mean the absolute world to me.
When you need me the most, know you mean the absolute world to me.
When you are not yourself, know you mean the absolute world to me.
When you feel alone, know you mean the absolute world to me.
When you face challenging days, I will walk alongside you and know you mean the absolute world to me.
If and when you need to vent, know you mean the absolute world to me.

If

What if my past comes flooding back.
What if my troubles come flooding around the corner.
What if my fears come looking for revenge.
What if my circumstances are at a standstill.

What if my denial is crumbling out.
What if my walls around me crack wide open.
What if my world comes crashing down around me.
What if I feel abandoned.

What if I feel unnoticed.
What if I feel reality is not what it seems.
What if a memory resurfaces.
What if I feel I am going to make a success of myself.

What if I lean on people close to and beside me.
What if I sense the worst.
What if I fall hard as stone.

Never Change

When you look back at your fragile past, know I would never change you for who you are.
When you face you your lifelong fears, know I would never change you for who you are.
When you try and break your lifelong issues that affect you, know I would never change you for who you are.
When you try and overcome the loneliness you feel, know I would never change you for who you are.
When you feel down, know I would never change you for who you are.
If and when you feel broken, know I would never change you for who you are.
When you feel like you're in a dark place, know I would never change you for who you are.
When you feel like you're struggling, know I would never change you for who you are.

When your inner cries take its toll on you, know I would never change you for who you are.
When you don't feel strong enough, know I would never change you for who you are.
When you don't feel brave enough, know I would never change you for who you are.
When you feel low, know I would never change you for who you are.

When you feel lost in any way, know I would never change you for who you are.
When you need a shoulder to cry on, know I would never change you for who you are.
If and when you don't feel good enough, know I would never change you for who you are.
When you feel like an outsider, know I would never change you for who you are.

If and when you feel rejected, know I would never change you for who you are.
When you feel like giving up, know I would never change you for who you are.
If and when you feel unwanted, know I would never change you for who you are.
If and when you feel worthless, know I would never change you for who you are.

When you feel like you are entering an unknown trap, know I would never change you for who you are.
When you feel like you're in denial, know I would never change you for who you are.

If and when you have nowhere to turn, know I would never change you for who you are.
If and when you don't feel you have the courage to fight, know I would never change you for who you are.
If and when you feel insecure, know I would never change you for who you are.
If and when you feel guilt in any way, know I would never change you for who you are.
When you need me the most, know I would never change you for who you are.
When you are not yourself, know I would never change you for who you are.
When you feel alone, know I would never change you for who you are.
When you face challenging days, I will walk alongside you and know I would never change you for who you are.
If and when you need to vent, know I would never change you for who you are.

Wish

My only wish of my past becoming a distant memory in the back of my mind.
My only wish is to make my friends proud of me.
My only wish is to have the perfect year.
My only wish is to make my dreams a reality.

My only wish Is to have those who accept me for me around me.
My only wish is not to mess up.
My only wish is to spend time with the people in my life that don't see me as a failure.
My only wish is not to feel the pain.

My only wish is to feel free.
My only wish is to choose who I spend my time with.
My only wish is not to get hurt in any way.
My only wish is not to feel betrayed by anyone.

Up To You

When you look back at your fragile past, know I will always look up to you.
When you face your lifelong fears, know I will always look up to you.
When you try and break your lifelong issues that affect you, know I will always look up to you.
When you try and overcame the loneliness you feel, know I will always look up to you.

When you feel down, know I will always look up to you.
If and when you feel broken, know I will always look up to you.
When you feel like you're in a dark place, know I will always look up to you.
When you feel like you're struggling, know I will always look up to you.

When your inner cries take its toll on you, know I will always look up to you.
When you don't feel strong enough, know I will always look up to you.
When you don't feel brave enough, know I will always look up to you.
When you feel low, know I will always look up to you.

When you feel lost in any way, know I will always look up to you.
When you need a shoulder to cry on, know I will always look up to you.
If and when you don't feel good enough, know I will always look up to you.
When you feel like an outsider, know I will always look up to you.

If and when you feel rejected, know I will always look up to you.
When you feel like giving up, know I will always look up to you.
If and when you feel unwanted, know I will always look up to you.
If and when you feel worthless, know I will always look up to you.

When you feel like your entering an unknown trap, know I will always look up to you.
When you feel like you're in denial, know I will always
If and when you have nowhere to turn, know I will always look up to you.
If and when you feel you don't have the courage to fight, know I will always look up to you.

If and when you feel insecure, know I will always look up to you.
If and when you feel guilt in any way, know I will always look up to you.
When you need me the most, know I will always look up to you.
When you are not yourself, know I will always look up to you.
When you feel alone, know I will always look up to you.
When you face challenging days, I will walk alongside you and know I will always look up to you.
If and when you need to vent, know I will always look up to you.

A Star

You are a star in my mind.
You are a star in my reality.
You are a star in the way you thrive.
You are a star to me.

You are star quality.
You are a superstar in no uncertain ways.
You got the stardom in you.
You are the star that you wanna be.

You are a true star.
You are an amazing talented star.
You are an incredible star.
You are a fabulous star.

You are a tremendous star.
You are a spectacular star.
You are an awesome star.
You are an excellent star.

You are an extraordinary star.
You are a magnificent star.
You are a mega star.
You are a marvellous star.

You are the rarest star.
You are the most loyalist star.
You are the most genuine star.
You are a firestorm star.
You are a fiery star.
You are a Rock star to me.

Up To Me

When you look back at your fragile past, know you can always look up to me.
When you face your lifelong fears, know you can always look up to me.
When you try and break your lifelong issues that affect you, know you can always look up to you me.
When you try and overcame the loneliness you feel, know you can always look up to me.

When you feel down, know you can always look up to me.
If and when you feel broken, know you can always look up to me.
When you feel like you're in a dark place, know you can always look up to me.
When you feel like you're struggling, know you can always look up to me.

When your inner cries take its toll on you, know you can always look up to me.
When you don't feel strong enough, know you can always look up to me.
When you don't feel brave enough, know you can always look up to me.
When you feel low, know you can always look up to me.

When you feel lost in any way, know you can always look up to me.
When you need a shoulder to cry on, know you can always look up to me.
If and when you don't feel good enough, know you can always look up to me.
When you feel like an outsider, know you can always look up to me.

If and when you feel rejected, know you can always look up to me.
When you feel like giving up, know you can always look up to me.
If and when you feel unwanted, know you can always look up to me.
If and when you feel worthless, know you can always look up to me.

When you feel like your entering an unknown trap, know you can always look up to me.
When you feel like you're in denial, know you can always look up to me.
If and when you have nowhere to turn, know you can always look up to me.
If and when you feel you don't have the courage to fight, know you can always look up to me.
If and when you feel insecure, know you can always look up to me.
If and when you feel guilt in any way, know you can always look up to me.
When you need me the most, know you can always look up to me.
When you are not yourself, know you can always look up to me.
When you feel alone, know you can always look up to me.
When you face challenging days, I will walk alongside you and know you can always look up to me.
If and when you need to vent, know you can always look up to me.

Host

You are the best host.
You are an amazing host.
You are an awesome host.
You are a very very talented host.

You are a fabulous host.
You are a tremendous host.
You are a great host.
You are a perfect host.

You are an incredible host.
You are a fair host.
You are an excellent host.
You are an extraordinary host.

You are the host with the most.
You are a blast of a host.
You are a mega host.
You are a magnificent host.

You are a fantastic host.
You are a magical host
You are the host we love.
You are a natural host

You are a superior host.
You are a brilliant host.
You are an epic host.
You are a spectacular host.
You are a trouper of a host.
You are a super genius host.
You were born to be a host.
You are a passionate host.
You are a carefree host.
You are a loyal host.
You are an inspirational host.

Your Shell

When you look back at your fragile past, know I will always try and bring you out of your shell.
When you face your lifelong fears, know I will always try and bring you out of your shell.
When you try and break your lifelong issues that affect you, know I will always try and bring you out of your shell.
When you try and overcame the loneliness you feel, know I will always try and bring you out of your shell.

When you feel down, know I will always try and bring you out of your shell.
If and when you feel broken, know I will always try and bring you out of your shell.
When you feel like you're in a dark place, know I will always try and bring you out of your shell.
When you feel like you're struggling, know I will always try and bring you out of your shell.

When your inner cries take its toll on you, know I will always try and bring you out of your shell.
When you don't feel strong enough, know I will always try and bring you out of your shell.
When you don't feel brave enough, know I will always try and bring you out of your shell.
When you feel low, know I will always try and bring you out of your shell.

When you feel lost in any way, know I will always try and bring you out of your shell.
When you need a shoulder to cry on, know I will always try and bring you out of your shell.
If and when you don't feel good enough, know I will always try and bring you out of your shell.
When you feel like an outsider, know I will always try and bring you out of your shell.

If and when you feel rejected, know I will always try and bring you out of your shell.
When you feel like giving up, know I will always try and bring you out of your shell.
If and when you feel unwanted, know I will always try and bring you out of your shell.

If and when you feel worthless, know I will always try and bring you out of your shell.

When you feel like your entering an unknown trap, know I will always try and bring you out of your shell.
When you feel like you're in denial, know I will always try and bring you out of your shell.
If and when you have nowhere to turn, know I will always try and bring you out of your shell.
If and when you feel you don't have the courage to fight, know I will always try and bring you out of your shell.
If and when you feel insecure, know I will always try and bring you out of your shell.
If and when you feel guilt in any way, know I will always try and bring you out of your shell.
When you need me the most, know I will always try and bring you out of your shell.
When you are not yourself, know I will always try and bring you out of your shell.
When you feel alone, know I will always try always try and bring you out of your shell.
When you face challenging days, I will walk alongside you and know I will always try and bring you out of your shell.
If and when you need to vent, know I will always try and bring you out of your shell.

Admire

When you look back at your fragile past, know I will always admire you.
When you face your lifelong fears, know I will always admire you.
When you try and break your lifelong issues that affect you, know I will always admire you.
When you try and overcame the loneliness you feel, know I will always admire you.

When you feel down, know I will always admire you.
If and when you feel broken, know I will always admire you.
When you feel like you're in a dark place, know I will always admire you.
When you feel like you're struggling, know I will always admire you.

When your inner cries take its toll on you, know I will always admire you.
When you don't feel strong enough, know I will always admire you.
When you don't feel brave enough, know I will always admire you
When you feel low, know I will always admire you.

When you feel lost in any way, know I will always admire you.
When you need a shoulder to cry on, know I will always admire you.
If and when you don't feel good enough, know I will always admire you.
When you feel like an outsider, know I will always admire you.

If and when you feel rejected, know I will always admire you.
When you feel like giving up, know I will always admire you.
If and when you feel unwanted, know I will always admire you.
If and when you feel worthless, know I will always admire you

When you feel like your entering an unknown trap, know I will always admire you.
When you feel like you're in denial, know I will always admire you.
If and when you have nowhere to turn, know I will always admire you.
If and when you feel you don't have the courage to fight, know I will always admire you.
If and when you feel insecure, know I will always admire you.
If and when you feel guilt in any way, know I will always admire you.
When you need me the most, know I will always admire you.
When you are not yourself, know I will always admire you.
When you feel alone, know I will always admire you.
When you face challenging days, I will walk alongside you and know I will always admire you.
If and when you need to vent, know I will always admire you.

Cling

Never cling on to ur fragile past.
Never cling on to ur energetic demons.
Never cling on to ur troubles that cast a doubt.
Never cling on to difficult times they will only drag you down.

Never cling on to the people that want you to drown and fail.
Never cling on to the people that don't see the best in you.
Never cling on to the people that try and break you.
Never cling on to the people who show hatred at how well you do in life.

Never cling on to anger it will destroy you.
Never cling on to bitterness it will always find a way to keep you from moving on.
Never cling on to people you ghost from ur life.
Never cling on to the people who don't wanna see you thrive.

Never cling on to the people who don't see you for you.
Never cling on to the people that judge you.
Never cling on to ur emotional strain it will only make you miserable.

Always cling on to the people that are close to you and stand with you no matter what.

The Warrior

When you look back at your fragile past, know I will always bring out the warrior in you.
When you face your lifelong fears, know I will always bring out the warrior in you.
When you try and break your lifelong issues that affect you, know I will always bring out the warrior in you.
When you try and overcame the loneliness you feel, know I will always bring out the warrior in you.

When you feel down, know I will always bring out the warrior in you.
If and when you feel broken, know I will always bring out the warrior in you.
When you feel like you're in a dark place, know I will always bring out the warrior in you.
When you feel like you're struggling, know I will always bring out the warrior in you.

When your inner cries take its toll on you, know I will always bring out the warrior in you.
When you don't feel strong enough, know I will always bring out the warrior in you.
When you don't feel brave enough, know I will always bring out the warrior in you.
When you feel low, know I will always bring out the warrior in you.

When you feel lost in any way, know I will always bring out the warrior in you.
When you need a shoulder to cry on, know I will always bring out the warrior in you.
If and when you don't feel good enough, know I will always bring out the warrior in you.
When you feel like an outsider, know I will always bring out the warrior in you.

If and when you feel rejected, know I will always bring out the warrior in you.
When you feel like giving up, know I will always bring out the warrior in you.
If and when you feel unwanted, know I will always bring out the warrior in you.
If and when you feel worthless, know I will always bring out the warrior in you.

When you feel like your entering an unknown trap, know I will always bring out the warrior in you.
When you feel like you're in denial, know I will always bring out the warrior in you.

If and when you have nowhere to turn, know I will always bring out the warrior in you.
If and when you feel you don't have the courage to fight, know I will always bring out the warrior in you.
If and when you feel insecure, know I will always bring out the warrior in you.
If and when you feel guilt in any way, know I will always bring out the warrior in you.
When you need me the most, know I will always bring out the warrior in you.
When you are not yourself, know I will always bring out the warrior in you.
When you feel alone, know I will always bring out the warrior in you.
When you face challenging days, I will walk alongside you and know I will always bring out the warrior in you.
If and when you need to vent, know I will always bring out the warrior in you.

Drown

Let me drown the past out.
Let me drown the troubles that follow me.
Let me drown out the hurtful remarks that come my way.
Let me drown out the hurtful words that make me feel like a nobody.

Let me drown out the way I was.
Let me drown out the endless games some people play with my emotions.
Let me drown out the endless resentment I feel.
Let me drown out the pain that comes my way.
Let me drown out the endless mind games some people won't let me forget.

Screw

When you look back at your fragile past, know I will never let anyone screw you over.
When you face your lifelong fears, know I will never let anyone screw you over.
When you try and break your lifelong issues that affect you, know I will never let anyone screw you over.
When you try and overcame the loneliness you feel, know I will never let anyone screw you over.

When you feel down, know I will never let anyone screw you over.
If and when you feel broken, know I will never let anyone screw you over.
When you feel like you're in a dark place, know I will never let anyone screw you over.
When you feel like you're struggling, know I will never let anyone screw you over.

When your inner cries take its toll on you, know I will never let anyone screw you over.
When you don't feel strong enough, know I will never let anyone screw you over.
When you don't feel brave enough, know I will never let anyone screw you over.
When you feel low, know I will never let anyone screw you over.

When you feel lost in any way, know I will never let anyone screw you over.
When you need a shoulder to cry on, know I will never let anyone screw you over.
If and when you don't feel good enough, know I will never let anyone screw you over.
When you feel like an outsider, know I will never let anyone screw you over.

If and when you feel rejected, know I will never let anyone screw you over
When you feel like giving up, know I will never let anyone screw you over.
If and when you feel unwanted, know I will never let anyone screw you over.
If and when you feel worthless, know I will never let anyone screw you over.

When you feel like your entering an unknown trap, know I will never let anyone screw you over.
When you feel like you're in denial, know I will never let anyone screw you over.
If and when you have nowhere to turn, know I will never let anyone screw you over.

If and when you feel you don't have the courage to fight, know I will never let anyone screw you over.

If and when you feel insecure, know I will never let anyone screw you over.
If and when you feel guilt in any way, know I will never let anyone screw you over.
When you need me the most, know I will never let anyone screw you over.
When you are not yourself, know I will never let anyone screw you over.
When you feel alone, know I will never let anyone screw you over.
When you face challenging days, I will walk alongside you and know I will never let anyone screw you over.
If and when you need to vent, know I will never let anyone screw you over.

Eliminate

You eliminate my past.
You eliminate my pain.
You eliminate my lifelong fears.
You eliminate my underlying issues.

You eliminate my energetic demons.
You eliminate my loneliness.
You eliminate my sadness.
You eliminate my rage.

You eliminate the blame I hold within.
You eliminate my nightmares.
You eliminate my obstacles that are in my way.
You eliminate whatever comes my way.

You eliminate any betrayal that comes my way.
You eliminate my bad memories.
You eliminate my bad experiences.
You eliminate my frowns and replace them with a smile.

You eliminate my emotions that drag me down and you lift my spirits.
You eliminate my darkest days and brighten them up.
You eliminate my darkest moments and light it up like no other.
You eliminate my inner crisis and help me defy them.
You eliminate the long rollercoaster I have been on.
You eliminate the long road I walk down.

The Best

When you look back at your fragile past, know I will always bring out the best in you.
When you face your lifelong fears, know I will always bring out the best in you.
When you try and break your lifelong issues that affect you, know I will always bring out the best in you.
When you try and overcame the loneliness you feel, know I will always bring out the best in you.

When you feel down, know I will always bring out the best in you.
If and when you feel broken, know I will always bring out the best in you.
When you feel like you're in a dark place, know I will always bring out the best in you.
When you feel like you're struggling, know I will always bring out the best in you.

When your inner cries take its toll on you, know I will always bring out the best in you.
When you don't feel strong enough, know I will always bring out the best in you.
When you don't feel brave enough, know I will always bring out the best in you.
When you feel low, know I will always bring out the best in you.

When you feel lost in any way, know I will always bring out the best in you.
When you need a shoulder to cry on, know I will always bring out the best in you.
If and when you don't feel good enough, know I will always bring out the best in you.
When you feel like an outsider, know I will always bring out the best in you.

If and when you feel rejected, know I will always bring out the best in you.
When you feel like giving up, know I will always bring out the best in you.
If and when you feel unwanted, know I will always bring out the best in you.
If and when you feel worthless, know I will always bring out the best in you.

When you feel like your entering an unknown trap, know I will always bring out the best in you.
When you feel like you're in denial, know I will always bring out the best in you.
If and when you have nowhere to turn, know I will always bring out the best in you.

If and when you feel you don't have the courage to fight, know I will always bring out the best in you.

If and when you feel insecure, know I will always bring out the best in you.
If and when you feel guilt in any way, know I will always bring out the best in you.
When you need me the most, know I will always bring out the best in you.
When you are not yourself, know I will always bring out the best in you.
When you feel alone, know I will always bring out the best in you.
When you face challenging days, I will walk alongside you and know I will always bring out the best in you.
If and when you need to vent, know I will always bring out the best in you.

Let My Voice

Let my voice be a way of telling you how much you mean to me.
Let my voice be a little reminder of how I wanna be.
Let my voice be true to those around me.
Let my voice be my reaction to things I've had to keep to myself.
Let my voice be the answer to your uncertainty.
Let my voice be the one to give you reassurance about what you feel within.

Perfect

When you look back at your fragile past, know you are perfect to me.
When you face your lifelong fears, know you are perfect to me.
When you try and break your lifelong issues that affect you, know you are perfect to me.
When you try and overcame the loneliness you feel, know you are perfect to me.

When you feel down, know you are perfect to me.
If and when you feel broken, know you are perfect to me.
When you feel like you're in a dark place, know you are perfect to me.
When you feel like you're struggling, know you are perfect to me.

When your inner cries take its toll on you, know you are perfect to me.
When you don't feel strong enough, know you are perfect to me.
When you don't feel brave enough, know you are perfect to me.
When you feel low, know you are perfect to me.
When you feel lost in any way, know you are perfect to me.
When you need a shoulder to cry on, know you are perfect to me.
If and when you don't feel good enough, know you are perfect to me.
When you feel like an outsider, know you are perfect to me.

If and when you feel rejected, know you are perfect to me.
When you feel like giving up, know you are perfect to me.
If and when you feel unwanted, know you are perfect to me.
If and when you feel worthless, know you are perfect to me.

When you feel like your entering an unknown trap, know you are perfect to me
When you feel like you're in denial, know you are perfect to me.
If and when you have nowhere to turn, know you are perfect to me.
If and when you feel you don't have the courage to fight, know you are perfect to me.
if and when you feel insecure, know you are perfect to me.
If and when you feel guilt in any way, know you are perfect to me.
When you need me the most, know you are perfect to me.
When you are not yourself, know you are perfect to me.
When you feel alone, know you are perfect to me.
When you face challenging days, I will walk alongside you and know you are perfect to me.
If and when you need to vent, know you are perfect to me.

Over You

When you look back at your fragile past, know I will never let anyone walk all over you.
When you face your lifelong fears, know I will never let anyone walk all over you.
When you try and break your lifelong issues that affect you, know I will never let anyone walk all over you.
When you try and overcame the loneliness you feel, know I will never let anyone walk all over you.

When you feel down, know I will never let anyone walk all over you.
If and when you feel broken, know I will never let anyone walk all over you.
When you feel like you're in a dark place, know I will never let anyone walk all over you.
When you feel like you're struggling, know I will never let anyone walk all over you.

When your inner cries take its toll on you, know I will never let anyone walk all over you.
When you don't feel strong enough, know I will never let anyone walk all over you.
When you don't feel brave enough, know I will never let anyone walk all over you.
When you feel low, know I will never let anyone walk all over you.

When you feel lost in any way, know I will never let anyone walk all over you.
When you need a shoulder to cry on, know I will never let anyone walk all over you.
If and when you don't feel good enough, know I will never let anyone walk all over you.
When you feel like an outsider, know I will never let anyone walk all over you.

If and when you feel rejected, know I will never let anyone walk all over you.
When you feel like giving up, know I will never let anyone walk all over you.
If and when you feel unwanted, know I will never let anyone walk all over you.
If and when you feel worthless, know I will never let anyone walk all over you.

When you feel like your entering an unknown trap, know I will never let anyone walk all over you.
When you feel like you're in denial, know I will never let anyone walk all over you.

If and when you have nowhere to turn, know I will never let anyone walk all over you.
If and when you feel you don't have the courage to fight, know I will never let anyone walk all over you.
If and when you feel insecure, know I will never let anyone walk all over you.
If and when you feel guilt in any way, know I will never let anyone walk all over you.
When you need me the most, know I will never let anyone walk all over you.
When you are not yourself, know I will never let anyone walk all over you.
When you feel alone, know I will never let anyone walk all over you.
When you face challenging days, I will walk alongside you and know I will never let anyone walk all over you.
If and when you need to vent, know I will never let anyone walk all over you.

The Worst

When you look back at your fragile past, know I will never let anyone bring out the worst in you.
When you face your lifelong fears, know I will never let anyone bring out the worst in you.
When you try and break your lifelong issues that affect you, know I will never let anyone bring out the worst in you.
When you try and overcame the loneliness you feel, know I will never let anyone bring out the worst in you.

When you feel down, know I will never let anyone bring out the worst in you.
If and when you feel broken, know I will never let anyone bring out the worst in you.
When you feel like you're in a dark place, know I will never let anyone bring out the worst in you.
When you feel like you're struggling, know I will never let anyone bring out the worst in you.

When your inner cries take its toll on you, know I will never let anyone bring out the worst in you.
When you don't feel strong enough, know I will never let anyone bring out the worst in you.
When you don't feel brave enough, know I will never let anyone bring out the worst in you.
When you feel low, know I will never let anyone bring out the worst in you.

When you feel lost in any way, know I will never let anyone bring out the worst in you.
When you need a shoulder to cry on, know I will never let anyone bring out the worst in you.
If and when you don't feel good enough, know I will never let anyone bring out the worst in you.
When you feel like an outsider, know I will never let anyone bring out the worst in you.

If and when you feel rejected, know I will never let anyone bring out the worst in you.
When you feel like giving up, know I will never let anyone bring out the worst in you.
If and when you feel unwanted, know I will never let anyone bring out the worst in you.

If and when you feel worthless, know I will never let anyone bring out the worst in you.

When you feel like your entering an unknown trap, know I will never let anyone bring out the worst in you
When you feel like you're in denial, know I will never let anyone bring out the worst in you.
If and when you have nowhere to turn, know I will never let anyone bring out the worst in you.
If and when you feel you don't have the courage to fight, know I will never let anyone bring out the worst in you.
If and when you feel insecure, know I will never let anyone bring out the worst in you.
If and when you feel guilt in any way, know I will never let anyone bring out the worst in you.
When you need me the most, know I will never let anyone bring out the worst in you
When you are not yourself, know I will never let anyone bring out the worst in you.
When you feel alone, know I will never let anyone bring out the worst in you.
When you face challenging days, I will walk alongside you and know I will never let anyone bring out the worst in you.
If and when you need to vent, know I will never let anyone bring out the worst in you.

Walk On Fire

When you look back at your fragile past, know I will always walk on fire for you.
When you face your lifelong fears, know I will always walk on fire for you.
When you try and break your lifelong issues that affect you, know I will always walk on fire for you.
When you try and overcame the loneliness you feel, know I will always walk on fire for you.

When you feel down, know I will always walk on fire for you.
If and when you feel broken, know I will always walk on fire for you.
When you feel like you're in a dark place, know I will always walk on fire for you.
When you feel like you're struggling, know I will always walk on fire for you.

When your inner cries take its toll on you, know I will always walk on fire for you.
When you don't feel strong enough, know I will always walk on fire for you.
When you don't feel brave enough, know I will always walk on fire for you
When you feel low, know I will always walk on fire for you.

When you feel lost in any way, know I will always walk on fire for you.
When you need a shoulder to cry on, know I will always walk on fire for you.
If and when you don't feel good enough, know I will always walk on fire for you.
When you feel like an outsider, know I will always walk on fire for you.

If and when you feel rejected, know I will always walk on fire for you.
When you feel like giving up, know I will always walk on fire for you.
If and when you feel unwanted, know I will always walk on fire for you.
If and when you feel worthless, know I will always walk on fire for you.

When you feel like your entering an unknown trap, know I will always walk on fire for you.
When you feel like you're in denial, know I will always walk on fire for you
If and when you have nowhere to turn, know I will always walk on fire for you.
If and when you feel you don't have the courage to fight, know I will always walk on fire for you.
If and when you feel insecure, know I will always walk on fire for you.
If and when you feel guilt in any way, know I will always walk on fire for you.
When you need me the most, know I will always walk on fire for you.

When you are not yourself, know I will always walk on fire for you.
When you feel alone, know I will always walk on fire for you.
When you face challenging days, I will walk alongside you and know I will always walk on fire for you.
If and when you need to vent, know I will always walk on fire for you.

Errors

Errors of my past don’t define me.
Errors of my fearless fears won’t stop me confronting them.
Errors of my underlying issues don’t have a hold on me.
Errors of my unexpected consequences will not redirect me.

Errors of hatred wont boil over me.
Errors of my ways won’t let me hit the ground.
Errors of my darkest moments will not let me go underground.

Never

When you look back at your fragile past, know I will never run a mile.
When you face your lifelong fears, know I will never run a mile.
When you try and break your lifelong issues that affect you, know I will never run a mile.
When you try and overcame the loneliness you feel, know I will never run a mile.

When you feel down, know I will never run a mile.
If and when you feel broken, know I will never run a mile.
When you feel like you're in a dark place, know I will never run a mile.
When you feel like you're struggling, know I will never run a mile.

When your inner cries take its toll on you, know I will never run a mile.
When you don't feel strong enough, know I will never run a mile.
When you don't feel brave enough, know I will never run a mile.
When you feel low, know I will never run a mile.

When you feel lost in any way, know I will never run a mile.
When you need a shoulder to cry on, know I will never run a mile.
If and when you don't feel good enough, know I will never run a mile.
When you feel like an outsider, know I will never run a mile.

If and when you feel rejected, know I will never run a mile.
When you feel like giving up, know I will never run a mile.
If and when you feel unwanted, know I will never run a mile.
If and when you feel worthless, know I will never run a mile.

When you feel like your entering an unknown trap, know I will never run a mile.
When you feel like you're in denial, know I will never run a mile.
If and when you have nowhere to turn, know I will never run a mile.
If and when you feel you don't have the courage to fight, know I will never run a mile.

If and when you feel insecure, know I will never run a mile.
If and when you feel guilt in any way, know I will never run a mile.
When you need me the most, know I will never run a mile.
When you are not yourself, know I will never run a mile.
When you feel alone, know I will never run a mile.
When you face challenging days, I will walk alongside you and know I will never run a mile.
If and when you need to vent, know I will never run a mile.

Extra Mile

When you look back at your fragile past, know I will go that extra mile for you.

When you face your lifelong fears, know I will go that extra mile for you.
When you try and break your lifelong issues that affect you, know I will go that extra mile for you.
When you try and overcame the loneliness you feel, know I will go that extra mile for you

When you feel down, know I will go that extra mile for you.
If and when you feel broken, know I will go that extra mile for you.
When you feel like you're in a dark place, know I will go that extra mile for you.
When you feel like you're struggling, know I will go that extra mile for you.

When your inner cries take its toll on you, know I will go that extra mile for you.
When you don't feel strong enough, know I will go that extra mile for you.
When you don't feel brave enough, know I will go that extra mile for you.
When you feel low, know I will go that extra mile for you.

When you feel lost in any way, know I will go that extra mile for you.
When you need a shoulder to cry on, know I will go that extra mile for you.
If and when you don't feel good enough, know I will go that extra mile for you.
When you feel like an outsider, know I will go that extra mile for you.

If and when you feel rejected, know I will go that extra mile for you.
When you feel like giving up, know I will go that extra mile for you.
If and when you feel unwanted, know I will go that extra mile for you.
If and when you feel worthless, know I will go that extra mile for you.

When you feel like your entering an unknown trap, know I will go that extra mile for you.
When you feel like you're in denial, know I will go that extra mile for you.
If and when you have nowhere to turn, know I will go that extra mile for you.
If and when you feel you don't have the courage to fight, know I will go that extra mile for you.

If and when you feel insecure, know I will go that extra mile for you.
If and when you feel guilt in any way, know I will go that extra mile for you.
When you need me the most, know I will go that extra mile for you.
When you are not yourself, know I will go that extra mile for you
When you feel alone, know I will go that extra mile for you.
When you face challenging days, I will walk alongside you and know I will go that extra mile for you.
If and when you need to vent, know I will go that extra mile for you.

Intentions

When you look back at your fragile past, know I will always have the best intentions for you.
When you face your lifelong fears, know I will always have the best intentions for you.
When you try and break your lifelong issues that affect you, know I will always have the best intentions for you.
When you try and overcame the loneliness you feel, know I will always have the best intentions for you.

When you feel down, know I will always have the best intentions for you.
If and when you feel broken, know I will always have the best intentions for you.
When you feel like you're in a dark place, know I will always have the best intentions for you.
When you feel like you're struggling, know I will always have the best intentions for you.

When your inner cries take its toll on you, know I will always have the best intentions for you.
When you don't feel strong enough, know I will always have the best intentions for you.
When you don't feel brave enough, know I will always have the best intentions for you.
When you feel low, know I will always have the best intentions for you.

When you feel lost in any way, know I will always have the best intentions for you.
When you need a shoulder to cry on, know I will always have the best intentions for you.
If and when you don't feel good enough, know I will always have the best intentions for you.
When you feel like an outsider, know I will always have the best intentions for you.

If and when you feel rejected, know I will always have the best intentions for you.
When you feel like giving up, know I will always have the best intentions for you.
If and when you feel unwanted, know I will always have the best intentions for you.

If and when you feel worthless, know I will always have the best intentions for you.
When you feel like your entering an unknown trap, know I will always have the best intentions for you.
When you feel like you're in denial, know I will always have the best intentions for you.
If and when you have nowhere to turn, know I will always have the best intentions for you.
If and when you feel you don't have the courage to fight, know I will always have the best intentions for you.

If and when you feel insecure, know I will always have the best intentions for you.
If and when you feel guilt in any way, know I will always have the best intentions for you.
When you need me the most, know I will always have the best intentions for you.
When you are not yourself, know I will always have the best intentions for you
When you feel alone, know I will always have the best intentions for you.
When you face challenging days, I will walk alongside you and know I will always have the best intentions for you.
If and when you need to vent, know I will always have the best intentions for you.

Interest

When you look back at your fragile past, know I will always have your best interest at heart.
When you face your lifelong fears, know I will always have your best interest at heart.
When you try and break your lifelong issues that affect you, know I will always have your best interest at heart.
When you try and overcame the loneliness you feel, know I will always have your best interest at heart.

When you feel down, know I will always have your best interest at heart.
If and when you feel broken, know I will always have your best interest at heart.
When you feel like you're in a dark place, know I will always have your best interest at heart.
When you feel like you're struggling, know I will always have your best interest at heart.

When your inner cries take its toll on you, know I will always have your best interest at heart.
When you don't feel strong enough, know I will always have your best interest at heart.
When you don't feel brave enough, know I will always have your best interest at heart.
When you feel low, know I will always have your best interest at heart.

When you feel lost in any way, know I will always have your best interest at heart.
When you need a shoulder to cry on, know I will always have your best interest at heart.
If and when you don't feel good enough, know I will always have your best interest at heart.
When you feel like an outsider, know I will always have your best interest at heart.

If and when you feel rejected, know I will always have your best interest at heart.
When you feel like giving up, know I will always have your best interest at heart.
If and when you feel unwanted, know I will always have your best interest at heart.
If and when you feel worthless, know I will always have your best interest at heart.

When you feel like your entering an unknown trap, know I will always have your best interest at heart.
When you feel like you're in denial, know I will always have your best interest at heart.
If and when you have nowhere to turn, know I will always have your best interest at heart.
If and when you feel you don't have the courage to fight, know I will always have your best interest at heart.
If and when you feel insecure, know I will always have your best interest at heart.
If and when you feel guilt in any way, know I will always have your best interest at heart.
When you need me the most, know I will always have your best interest at heart.
When you are not yourself, know I will always have your best interest at heart.
When you feel alone, know I will always have your best interest at heart.
When you face challenging days, I will walk alongside you and know I will always have your best interest at heart.
If and when you need to vent, know I will always have your best interest at heart.

B F

Ur my amazing best friend.
Ur my incredible best friend.
Ur my great best friend.
Ur my fantastic best friend.

Ur my fabulous best friend.
Ur my excellent best friend.
Ur my extraordinary best friend.
Ur my magnificent best friend.

Ur my golden best friend.
Ur my genuine best friend.
Ur my best friend forever.
Ur my one in a million best friend.

Ur my tremendous best friend.
Ur my true best friend.
Ur my best friend that never lets me go though rough times alone.
Ur my best friend that will not let me walk alone and will always walk with me.

Ur my best friend that sees me at my lowest point.
Ur my best friend that will help me in my hour of need.
Ur my best friend who helps me beat my battles.
Ur my best friend who never judges me for who I am.

Ur my best friend who takes me as I am.
Ur my best friend who lets me wipe my tears on you.
Ur my truthful best friend.
Ur my best friend who won’t let me fall to the ground.
Ur my best friend who wants to see the best in me.
Ur my best friend who don’t wanna see me fail.
Ur my best friend for life.

Hero

You are my hero helping me to process my fragile past.
You are my hero helping me to oversee my fearless fears head on.
You are my hero helping me to overcome my overturn of troubles that follow me.
You are my hero helping me to rise above my difficulties.

You are my hero in no uncertain ways.
You are my hero helping me to overshadow my doubts in my mind.
You are my hero helping me turn the various things that make a barrier.
You are my hero helping me stay on the straight and narrow.

You are my hero helping me to redirect my energy in a way that is used in a good way.
You are my hero helping me to realise my purpose.
You are my hero helping me turn my negativity in to a positive.
You are my hero helping me to realise my dreams.

You are my hero helping me to get the real me to shine.
You are my hero helping me to get the true me to light up.
You are my hero lighting up my smile any way you can.
You are my hero helping me through my darkest moments.

You are my hero helping me find answers to unknown questions I have.
You are my hero helping me by having such a massive heart of gold.
You are my hero helping me by having an massive impact on me and my life.
You are my hero helping me by having such a massive influence on me and my life.
You are my amazing hero; You are my inspirational hero.
You are my tremendous hero; You are my outstanding hero.

You are my extraordinary hero; You are my fabulous hero.
You are my fantastic hero; You are my hero in my reality.

You are my hero helping me to see that not everyone is as genuine as you.
You are my hero in keeping me calm in situations.
You are my loyal hero.
You are my hero just by being by my side.

You are my hero not letting me face anything alone.
You are my hero just by being you.
You are my hero because you brighten up my days.

Inspiration

You are my incredible inspiration.
You are my amazing inspiration.
You are my fabulous inspiration.
You are my never ending inspiration.

You are my epic inspiration.
You are my one in a million inspiration.
You are my awesome inspiration.
You are my extraordinary inspiration.

You are my true inspiration.
You are my tremendous inspiration.
You are my only inspiration.
You are my outstanding inspiration.

You are my lucky inspiration.
You are my unstoppable inspiration.
You are my forever inspiration.
You are my loyal inspiration.

You are my best inspiration.
You are my wonderful inspiration.
You are my superhero inspiration.
You are my supportive inspiration.

You are my kind hearted inspiration.
You are my golden inspiration.
You are my true natured inspiration.
You are my superstar inspiration.
You are my inseparable inspiration.
You are my inspiration through my reality.
You are my inspiration as you watch me thrive.
You are my inspiration in my mind.

Human Being

You are an amazing human being.
You are an incredible human being.
You are an excellent human being.
You are an extraordinary human being.

You are a carefree human being.
You are a rare human being.
You are an tremendous human being.
You are a kind hearted human being.

You are a huge inspirational human being.
You are the best human being.
You are a go getter human being.
You are a wonderful human being.

You are a believer in making things a reality.
You are a genuine human being.
You are a soul searcher.
You are a truthful human being.

You are a diamond human being.
You are a protective human being.
You are a mega human being.
You are a one in a million human being.

You are a loyal human being.
You have a golden heart.
You are a trustworthy human being.
You are an unusual human being.

You are a unique human being.
You are a passionate human being.
You are a brilliant human being.
You are an awesome human being.
You are a spectacular human being.
You are a bright spark of a human being.

My Hand

You held my hand when I looked back at my fragile past.
You held my hand at the trouble I try and block out.
You held my hand through my toughest times.
You held my hand through the difficult pain.

You held my hands through the dark moments.
You held my hand through the battles I faced.
You held my hand through my challenging times.
You held my hand through my failures.

You held my hand as I fall hard.
You held my hand when I try and make a life for myself.
You held my hand as my world comes crashing down around me.
You held my hand when I am sad.

You held my hand when I thrive.
You held my hand when I wipe my tears on you.
You held my hand when I needed you the most.
You held my hand when I am at my worst.

You held my hand when I am at my lowest.
You held my hand at my weakest.
You held my hand as you never let me face anything alone.
You held my hand when you walk beside me.

You held my hand when I got knocked down.
You held my hand through my achievements.
You held my hand when I didn't have hope.
You held my hand when I didn't have strength.

You held my hand when I tried to give in.
You held my hand when I felt broken.
You held my hand when I tried to give up.
You held my hand and never let go.

For Me

You were there for me when I looked back at my fragile past.
You were there for me when I continued to confront my energetic demons.
You were there for me when I overcame lifelong fears.
You were there for me when I needed to vent.

You were there for me when I needed the support.
You were there for me when I needed to escape my reality.
You were there for me when I needed you the most.
You were there for me when I needed a shoulder to cry on

You were there for me when I needed the encouragement.
You were there for me when I struggled.
You were there for me when I was at my lowest.
You were there for me when I was at my weakest.

You were there for me when I needed you in my hour of need.
You were there for me when I wanted to let out a scream.
You were there for me when I wanted to explode.
You were there for me when I was sad.

You were there for me when I needed to let out rage.
You were there for me when I felt broken.
You were there for me when I needed to fight my inner cries.
You were there for me when I felt abandoned.

You were there for me when I felt alone.
You were there for me when I felt insecure.
You were there for me when I needed you to make a massive difference in me and my life.
You were there for me when I needed you to make a massive influence on me and my life.

You were there for me when I needed comfort.
You were there for me when I fall apart.
You were there for me when I faced my underlying issues.
You were there for me when I needed a hug.
You were there for me when I needed to find a way of being me.
You were there for me when I needed cheering up.
You were there for me when I felt unnoticed.
You were there for me when I felt let down by others.

You were there for me when I needed a laugh.

You were there for me when I needed to face a challenging day.
You are there for me when I am in crisis.
You are there for me when I am going through my hard times.
You are there for me when I face my worst.
You are there for me when I cry.
You are there for me when I needed you to make me smile.

Imperfections

Imperfections are not easy to find.
Imperfections are what make you.
Imperfections are not far from the truth.
Imperfections are not what define you.

Imperfections will not defeat you.
Imperfections are what you make them.
Imperfections are not a weakness.
These around you will accept your imperfections and take them as they see them.
Imperfections do not rule what those around you think about you.

Thank You

Thanks to you I can face my fragile past.
Thanks to you I can face my lifelong fears.
Thanks to you I can put my endless battles to the back of my mind.
Thanks to you I feel good enough.

Thanks to you I feel wanted.
Thanks to you I feel free.
Thanks to you I know I have people who care about me.
Thanks to you I feel endlessly happy.

Thanks to you I am following my dreams and making them a reality.
Thanks to you I feel valued by those who want me in their lives.
Thanks to you I don't feel low.
Thanks to you I make myself a success.

Thanks to you I realise I have a purpose.
Thanks to you I make a life for myself.
Thanks to you I realised I have a voice.
Thanks to you I feel I can be the person I wanna be.

Thanks to you I believe in myself.
Thanks to you I don't let people who I ghosted from my life walk all over me.
Thanks to you I have hope.
Thanks to you I have strength.

Thanks to you I am the best I can be as you bring out the best in me.
Thanks to you I am never alone.
Thanks to you I never feel lost.
Thanks to you I am so passionate about the things I can do.

Thanks to you I know I can do anything.
Thanks to you I have the best people around me.
Thanks to you I feel so much stronger.
Thanks to you I feel a lot more braver.
Thanks to you I am me.
Thanks to you I have a burning sensation.
Thanks to you I can achieve the things I want from life.
Thank you for being you

Thank you for being in my life.

Thank you for bringing out the real me.
Thank you for bringing out the true me.
Thank you for being so loyal to me.

Thank you for helping me find myself.
Thank you for encouraging me.
Thank you for always being there for me when I needed you the most.
Thank you for always being beside me.

Thank you for always making me smile.
Thank you for being my role model.
Thank you for being my rock.
Thank you from the bottom of my heart.

Fall Out

Fall out of my mind.
Fall out of my heart.
Fall out of my pain.
Fall out of my heartbreak.

Fall out of my heartache.
Fall out of my emotional strength.
Fall out of my emotional strain.
Fallout from the forbidden pathway.
Fallout from my weakness.
Fallout from my limitless limits.

Role Model.

You are an amazing role model to me.
You are an incredible role model to me.
You are an extraordinary role model to me.
You are an excellent role model to me.

You are a superior role model to me.
You are a fabulous role model to me.
You are a fantastic role model to me.
You are the best role model to me.

You are a tremendous role model to me.
You are a brilliant role model to me.
You are a mega role model to me.
You are a one in a million role model to me.

You are an outstanding role model to me.
You are a loyal role model to me.
You make such a massive impact on me and my life just by being a role model to me.
You make such a massive difference in me and my life just by being a role model to me.

You are a magnificent role to me.
You are a rare role model to me.
I admire you.
I look up to you.

I wanna be more and more like you.
You are a trouper of a role model to me.
You are an awesome role model to me.
You are an epic role model to me.
You are a wonderful role model to me.
You are an inspirational role model to me.
You are a spectacular role model to me.

My Back

You have always had my back from the very beginning.
You have had my back since we first met.
You have had my back for over 14 years.
You have had my back during my time at school.

You have had my back when I felt I couldn't face my fragile past.
You have had my back when I couldn't face my bullies.
You have had my back when I had low self-esteem.
You have had my back when I couldn't face my insecurities.

You have had my back when I needed you the most.
You have had my back when I felt alone.
You have had my back when I couldn't face my days at college.
You have had my back from day one.

You have had my back when I needed to escape.
You have never let me down not once.
You have guided me through things I didn't think I could get through.
You have made me a better person.

You have had my back through the pain I endured.
You have had my back when I was so fragile.
You have had my back when I wasn't myself.
You have had my back through the difficulties I faced throughout.

You have had my back since I needed a shoulder to cry on.
You have always had my back when I faced any challenges throughout the years.
You have had my back on so many occasions.
You have had my back when I needed a push in the right direction.

You have had my back when I was feeling low.
You have had my back when I lost my way.
You have had my back when I struggled.
You have had my back when I felt I couldn't go on.

You have had my back when I fall apart.
You have had my back when no one else but you understands me.
You have had my back even when I've been a nightmare.
You have had my back when I couldn't see what was best for me at the time.

You have had my back and never left my side.
You have had my back even when I wanted out.
You have had my back even given me a chance to express myself.
You have had my back just by making a massive impact on me and my life.

You have had my back just by showing me I have a voice and I will be heard.
You have had my back when I just wanted to hide away.
You have had my back just by making a massive difference in me and my life.
You have had my back just by being there for me no matter what.

You have had my back through difficult situations I faced.
You have had my back when I face my worst.
You have had my back when I didn't feel good enough.
You gave me the courage I needed.

You have had my back when I felt broken.
You have had my back when was feeling down.
You have had my back when I felt betrayed.
You have had my back when I felt I couldn't cope.

You have had my back when I didn't feel brave enough.
You have had my back when I didn't feel strong enough.
You had my back when I finally realised you are one of a kind.
You have had my back when I needed a hug.

You have had my back through everything.
You have had my back just by being so loyal to me.
You have had my back just by being in my life.
You have had my back just by being you.

You have had my back just by showing me I can stand my ground.
You have had my back just by showing me I can achieve my goals.
You have had my back just by showing me I can be me.
You have had my back just by showing me that I have confidence to be who I wanna be.

You have had my back just by showing me I can make a success of myself.
You have had my back just by letting me show you the true me.
You have had my back just by letting me show you the real me.
Nothing will ever break us apart.
I wouldn't be me if it wasn't for you.

Under Your Wing

You take me under your wing when I look back at my fragile past.
You take me under your wing when I face my lifelong fears.
You take me under my wing when I'm down.
You take me under your wing when I need you the most.

You take me under your wing to keep me on the straight and narrow.
You take me under your wing when I have nowhere to turn.
You take me under your wing when no one else understands me but you.
You take me under your wing when I go into a destructive mode.

You take me under your wing when no one else gives me a fair chance.
You take me under your wing when I feel like I'm hitting rock bottom.
You take me under your wing when I go through tough times.
You take me under your wing when I feel broken.

You take me under your wing when I feel like I'm lost.
You take me under your wing when I feel rejection from people around me.
You take me under your wing when I feel rage about to come out of me.
You take me under your wing and never let me face anything alone.
You take me under you wing to keep me smiling when no one else can.

You take me under your wing when I feel my life is going down a destructive road.
You take me under your wing when I feel let down by others around me.
You take me under your wing when I feel hurt.
You take me under your wing when I feel unnoticed.

You take me under your wing when I feel like I'm breaking into a thousand pieces.
You take me under your wing to prove to people I am worthy of being.
You take me under your wing when I feel abandoned.
You take under your wing to show people I can bring out the true me.
You take me under your wing as you bring out the best in me.
You take me under your wing as you believe in me when no one else did.
You take me under your wing to keep me from rebellion.
You take me under your wing as you stand by me no matter what.

You take me under your wing when you see me in my hour of need.
You take me under your wing when you see me at my weakest.
You take me under your wing when you see me at my lowest.
You take me under your wing when you see me in denial.

Approach

I can approach my fragile past in a different way as you stand by me.
I can approach my lifelong fears in a different way as you stand by me.
I can approach my pain in a different way as you stand by me.
I can approach my hurt in a different way as you stand by me.

I can approach my difficulties in a different way as you stand by me.
I can approach my traumas in a different way as you stand by me.
I can approach my darkest days in a different way as you stand by me.
I can approach my abandonment issues in a different way as you stand by me.

I can stay on the straight and narrow as you stand by me.
I can approach my hour of need in a different way as you stand by me.
I can approach my chances in a different way as you stand by me.
I can approach my rejections in a different way as you stand by me.

I can approach taking risks in a different way as you stand by me.
I can face anything and everything in a different way as you stand by me.
I can approach my battles in a different way as you stand by me.
I can approach denial in a different way as you stand by me.

I can approach my doubts in a different way as you stand by me.
I can approach bringing the true me to the surface as you stand by me.
I can approach challenges that come my way in a different way as you stand by me.
I can achieve my goals in a different way as you stand by me.

I can be me in a different way as you stand by me.
I can approach my reality in a different way as you stand by me.
I can approach the feeling of feeling broken in a different way as you stand by me.
I can approach my loneliness in a different way as you stand by me.

I can approach finding myself in a different way as you stand by me.
I can approach hearing hateful words in a different way as you stand by me.
I can approach being dragged down a destructive road in a different way as you stand by me.
I can approach going into a destructive mode in a different way as you stand by me.
I can approach the cruelty in this world in a different way as you stand by me.
I can approach being as strong as I can be in a different way as you stand by me.

I can approach being as brave as I can be in a different way as you stand by me.
I can approach turning to the people I care about in a different way as you stand by me.

I can approach knowing I have a flood of people around me in a different way as you stand by me.
I can approach dangerous areas in a different way as you stand by me.
I can approach facing danger in a different way as you stand by me.
I can approach the consequences of my actions good or bad in a different way as you stand by me.
I can approach my backlashes in a different way as you stand by me.
I can approach my own way of life in a different way as you stand by me.

Vision Impairment

I never let my vision impairment define me as a person.
I never let my vision impairment break me.
I never let my vision impairment.
I never let my vision impairment impact my emotions.

I never let my vision impairment dictate my outlook on life.
I never let my vision impairment lose a battle as I win every one of them.
I never let my vision impairment define who I am in myself.
I never let my vision impairment stop me achieving my goals in life.

I never let my vision impairment determine the way I should be.
I never let my vision impairment stop me chasing long awaited dreams and turning them into reality
I never let my vision impairment being stronger than I've ever been.
I never let my vision impairment keep me down.
I never let my vision impairment stop me being braver than ever before.
I never let my vision impairment change me
I never let my vision impairment determine my abilities and capabilities.

Living Proof

Living proof of my fragile past.
Living proof of my lifelong fears.
Living proof of my underlying issues.
Living proof of my pain.

Living proof of my heartbreak.
Living proof of my darkest days.
Living proof of my rage.
Living proof that I can make dreams a reality.

Living proof that I can change my life for the better.
Living proof I can take a chance on things.
Living proof I can take a risk on things.
Living proof I can control what life throws my way.

Living proof that even though I had a difficult start in life I can make something of myself.
Living proof I have a flood of people around me to lean on.
Living proof I can make a u turn
Living proof I can change the outcome on my life.

Living proof I have people in my life that want me for me.
Living proof I have people in my life that care about me
Living proof I have people in my life when I need them the most.
Living proof I am never alone.

Living proof I have someone to always turn to.
Living proof that I have people in my life that will make me smile when I am down
Living proof I have people in my life that will be there for me through thick and thin.
Living proof I have people who will be there for me no matter what.

Living proof I have people in my life that will be there for me in my hour of need.
Living proof I have people in my life that will be there for me in my darkest of days.
Living proof I have people in my life that will be there for me when I need to escape my reality.

Living proof I have people in my life that will be there for me when I need to scream.
Living proof I have people in my life that will be there for me when I want to let out rage.
Living proof I have people in my life that will be there for me when I am sad.
Living proof I have people in my life as and when I want to vent.
Living proof I have people in my life that will cheer me up when I need it.
Living proof I have people in my life that will be there for me when I need a laugh.

Living proof I have people in my life that will be there for me when I need to talk any time.
Living proof I have people in my life that will be there for me when I need a shoulder to cry on.
Living proof I have people in my life that will be there for me when I have a meltdown.
Living proof I have people in my life that will be there for me when I have a breakdown.

Living proof I have people in my life that will be there for me and not let me walk alone and will walk beside me.
Living proof I have people in my life that will be there for me when I feel broken
Living proof I have people in my life that will be there for me when I feel rejected
Living proof I have people in my life that will be there for me when I don’t feel valued by others.
Living proof I have people in my life that will be there for me when I feel let down by others around me.
Living proof I have people in my life that will be there for me when I lead my own life in my own unique way.

Light

When I look back at my fragile past you light me up.
When I face my lifelong fears that terrorise me to no end you light me up.
When I try and break my lifelong issues that affect me you light me up.
When I try and overcome my loneliness you light me up.

When mu unruly things happen it happens in true unforgettable style and you light me up.
When you find me down you find a way to light me up.
As you find me broken you never leave me until you light ne up.
When you find me in a dark place you take me aside and light me up.

When you find me struggling you sit beside me and talk with me until you light me up.
When my inner cries take its toll on me you light me up.
When I don't feel strong enough you light me up.
When I don't feel brave enough you light me up.

When I feel low you light me up.
When I feel lost you light me up.
When I want to cry you give me your shoulder to wipe my tears on and you light me up.
When I don't feel good enough you light me up.

When I say nothing you know and you do everything you can to light me up.
When I feel like an outsider you light me up.
When I feel rejected you light me up.
When I feel like giving up you turn it around and light me up.

When I feel unwanted you light me up.
When I feel worthless you light me up.
When I walk into a trap you pull me out and light me up.
When I feel like I'm in denial you light me up.

When I have nowhere to turn you light me up.
When I don't have the courage to fight you light me up.
When I feel insecure you light me up.
When I feel guilt you know how to make me smile and you light me up.
As you are my lifelong friend you light me up.
As I trust in you, you light me up.
When I feel tired you keep me going and you light me up.

When you take a risk on me you light me up.

When you take a chance on me you light me up.
When I am around you, you light me up.
When I go through challenging days you light me up.
When I go into a destructive mode you light me up.

When I feel alone you appear and light me up.
When I walk down a long road you walk beside me and light me up.
When I feel wonky you patch me up and light me up
You light up my life.
You light up my world.
When I am not myself you light me up any way you can.

Individuality

I am a determined individual.
I am a free individual that knows my mind.
I am an inspirational individual.
I am a strong individual.

I am true to the point individual.
I am an individual that says what's on my on my mind.
I am an individual who use to struggle.
I am an individual who is supportive.

I am an individual who will do anything to be heard.
I am an individual with a wild heart.
I am an individual who will never let anything get in the way of my dreams.
I am an individual with a tough outlook on life.

I am an individual not to be messed with.
I am an individual who is unique.
I am an individual if crossed will let out rage.
I am an individual that can let out a real temper.

I am an individual who won't be held back.
I am an individual that will take potential to the next level.
I am an unstoppable individual.

Apart

I won't let my fragile past tear me apart as long as I've got you.
I won't let my lifelong fears that terrorise me to no end tear me apart as long as I've got you.
I won't let my loneliness take its toll on me tear me apart as long as I've got you.
I won't let my rage that comes out of me tear me apart as long as I've got you.

I won't let my lifelong issues that affect me tear me apart as long as I've got you.
When you find me down, I won't let it tear me apart as long as I've got you.
When you find me broken, I won't let it tear me apart as long as I've got you,
When you find me in a dark place, I won't let it tear me apart as long as I've got you.

When you find me struggling, I won't let it tear me apart as long as I've got you,
When my inner cries take its toll on me, I won't let it tear me apart as long as I've got you.
When I don't feel strong enough, I won't let it tear me apart as long as I've got you.
When I don't feel brave enough, I won't let it tear me apart as long as I've got you.

When I feel low, I won't let it tear me apart as long as I've got you.
When I feel lost I won't let it tear me apart as long as I've got you.
When I wanna cry I won't let it tear me apart as long as I've got you.
When I don't feel good enough, I won't let it tear me apart as long as I've got you.

When I feel like an outsider, I won't let it tear me apart as long as I've got you.
When I feel rejected, I won't let it tear me apart as long as I've got you.
When I feel like giving up, I won't let it tear me apart as long as I've got you.
When I feel hurt, I won't let it tear me apart as long as I've got you.

When I feel damaged, I won't let it tear me apart as long as I've got you.
When I like there's a hole in me, I won't let it tear me apart as long as I've got you.
When I am not myself, I won't let it tear me apart as long as I've got you.
When I need you the most, I will call out and I won't let it tear me apart as long as I've got you.
When I feel torn, I won't let it tear me apart as long as I've got you.

Reach Out

When you look back at your fragile past you can reach out to me.
When you face your lifelong fears, you can reach out to me,
When try and break your lifelong issues that affect you, you can reach out to me,
When you try and overcome the loneliness you feel you can reach out to me.

When you feel down you can reach out to me.
If and when you feel broken you can reach out to me.
When you feel like you're in a dark place you can reach out to me.
When you feel like you're struggling you can reach out to me.

When your inner cries take its toll on you, you can reach out to me.
When you don't feel strong enough you can reach out to me.
When you don't feel brave enough you can reach out to me.
When you feel low you can reach out to me.

When you feel lost in any way you can reach out to me.
When you need a shoulder to cry on you can reach out to me.
If and when you don't feel good enough you can reach out to me.
When you feel like an outsider you can reach out to me.

If and when you feel rejected you can reach out to me.
When you feel like giving up you can reach out to me.
If and when you feel unwanted you can reach out to me.
If and when you feel worthless you can reach out to me.

When you feel like your entering an unknown trap you can reach out to me.
When you feel like you're in denial you can reach out to me.
If and when you have nowhere to turn you can reach out to me.
If and when you don't feel you have the courage to fight you can reach out to me.

If and when you feel insecure you can reach out to me.
If and when you feel guilt you can reach out to me.
When you need me the most you can reach out to me.
When you are not yourself you can reach out to me.
When you feel alone you can reach out to me.
When you face challenging days, I will walk along side you and you can reach out to me.
If and when you need to vent you can reach out to me.

Lean On

When you look back at your fragile past you can lean on me.
When you face your lifelong fears, you can lean on me.
When try and break your lifelong issues that affect you, you can lean on me.
When you try and overcome the loneliness you feel you can lean on me.

When you feel down you can lean on me.
If and when you feel broken you can lean on me.
When you feel like you're in a dark place you can lean on me.
When you feel like you're struggling you can lean on me.

When your inner cries take its toll on you, you can lean on me.
When you don't feel strong enough you can lean on me.
When you don't feel brave enough you can lean on me.
When you feel low you can lean on me.

When you feel lost in any way you can lean on me.
When you need a shoulder to cry on you can lean on me.
If and when you don't feel good enough you can lean on me.
When you feel like an outsider you can lean on me.

If and when you feel rejected you can lean on me.
When you feel like giving up you can lean on me.
If and when you feel unwanted you can lean on me.
If and when you feel worthless you can lean on me.

When you feel like your entering an unknown trap you can lean on me.
When you feel like you're in denial you can lean on me.
If and when you have nowhere to turn you can lean on me.
If and when you don't feel you have the courage to fight you can lean on me.

If and when you feel insecure you can lean on me.
If and when you feel guilt you can lean on me.
When you need me the most you can lean on me.
When you are not yourself you can lean on me.
When you feel alone you can lean on me
When you face challenging days, I will walk alongside you and you can lean on me.
If and when you need to vent you can lean on me.

Vent

When you look back at your fragile past you can vent to me.
When you face your lifelong fears, you can vent to me.
When try and break your lifelong issues that affect you, you can vent to me.
When you try and overcome the loneliness you feel you can vent to me.

When you feel down you can vent to me.
If and when you feel broken you can vent to me.
When you feel like you're in a dark place you can vent to me.
When you feel like you're struggling you can vent to me.

When your inner cries take its toll on you, you can vent to me.
When you don't feel strong enough you can vent to me.
When you don't feel brave enough you can vent to me.
When you feel low you can vent to me.

When you feel lost in any way you can vent to me.
When you need a shoulder to cry on you can vent to me.
If and when you don't feel good enough you can vent to me.
When you feel like an outsider you can vent to me.

If and when you feel rejected you can vent to me.
When you feel like giving up you can vent to me.
If and when you feel unwanted you can vent to me.
If and when you feel worthless you can vent to me.

When you feel like your entering an unknown trap you can vent to me.
When you feel like you're in denial you can vent to me.
If and when you have nowhere to turn you can vent to me.
If and when you don't feel you have the courage to fight you can vent to me.

If and when you feel insecure you can vent to me.
If and when you feel guilt you can vent to me.
When you need me the most you can vent to me.
When you are not yourself you can vent to me.

When you feel alone you can vent to me.
When you face challenging days, I will walk alongside you and you can vent to me.
If and when you need to vent you can vent to me.

Count

When you look back at your fragile past you can count on me
When you face your lifelong fears, you can count on me.
When try and break your lifelong issues that affect you, you can count on me.
When you try and overcome the loneliness you feel you can recount on me.

When you feel down you can count on me.
If and when you feel broken you can count on me.
When you feel like you're in a dark place you can count on me.
When you feel like you're struggling you can count on me.

When your inner cries take its toll on you, you can count on me.
When you don't feel strong enough you can count on me.
When you don't feel brave enough you can count on me.
When you feel low you can count on me.

When you feel lost in any way you can count on me.
When you need a shoulder to cry on you can count on me.
If and when you don't feel good enough you can count on me.
When you feel like an outsider you can count on me.

If and when you feel rejected you can count on me.
When you feel like giving up you can count on me.
If and when you feel unwanted you can count on me.
If and when you feel worthless you can count on me.

When you feel like your entering an unknown trap you can count on me.
When you feel like you're in denial you can count on me.
If and when you have nowhere to turn you can count on me.
If and when you don't feel you have the courage to fight you can count on me.

If and when you feel insecure you can count on me.
If and when you feel guilt you can count on me.
When you are not yourself you can count on me

When you feel alone you can count on me.
When you face challenging days, I will walk alongside you and you can count on me.
If and when you need to vent you can count on me.

Your Back

When you look back at your fragile past, I will have your back.
When you face your lifelong fears, I will have your back.
When try and break your lifelong issues that affect you, I will have your back.
When you try and overcome the loneliness you feel I will have your back.

When you feel down, I will have your back.
If and when you feel broken, I will have your back.
When you feel like you're in a dark place I will have your back.
When you feel like you're struggling I will have your back.

When your inner cries take its toll on you, I will have your back.
When you don't feel strong enough will have your back.
When you don't feel brave enough, I will have your back.
When you feel low, I will have your back.

When you feel lost in any way I will have your back
When you need a shoulder to cry on I will have your back.
If and when you don't feel good enough, I will have your back.
When you feel like an outsider, I will have your back.

If and when you feel rejected, I will have your back.
When you feel like giving up, I will have your back.
If and when you feel unwanted, I will have your back.
If and when you feel worthless, I will have your back.

When you feel like your entering an unknown trap, I will have your back.
When you feel like you're in denial, I will have your back.
If and when you have nowhere to turn, I will have your back.
If and when you don't feel you have the courage to fight, I will have your back.

If and when you feel insecure, I will have your back.
If and when you feel guilt, I will have your back,
When you need me the most, I will have your back.
When you are not yourself, I will have your back.

When you feel alone, I will have your back.
When you face challenging days, I will walk alongside you and I will have your back.
If and when you need to vent, I will have your back.

Rock

When you look back at your fragile past, I will be your rock.
When you face your lifelong fears, I will be your rock.
When try and break your lifelong issues that affect you, I will be your rock.
When you try and overcome the loneliness you feel I will be your rock.

When you feel down, I will be your rock.
If and when you feel broken, I will be your rock.
When you feel like you're in a dark place I will be your rock.
When you feel like you're struggling I will be your rock.

When your inner cries take its toll on you, I will be your rock,
When you don't feel strong enough will be your rock.
When you don't feel brave enough, I will be your rock.
When you feel low, I will be your rock.

When you feel lost in any way I will be your rock.
When you need a shoulder to cry on, I will be your rock.
If and when you don't feel good enough, I will be your rock,
When you feel like an outsider, I will be your rock.

If and when you feel rejected, I will be your rock.
When you feel like giving up, I will be your rock.
If and when you feel unwanted, I will be your rock.
If and when you feel worthless, I will be your rock.

When you feel like your entering an unknown trap, I will be your rock.
When you feel like you're in denial, I will be your rock.
If and when you have nowhere to turn, I will be your rock,
If and when you don't feel you have the courage to fight, I will be your rock,

If and when you feel insecure, I will be your rock
If and when you feel guilt, I will be your rock.
When you need me the most, I will be your rock.
When you are not yourself, I will be your rock.
When you feel alone, I will be your rock.
When you face challenging days, I will walk alongside you and I will be your rock.
If and when you need to vent, I will be your rock.

Rely

When you look back at your fragile past, you can always rely on me.
When you face your lifelong fears, you can always rely on me.
When try and break your lifelong issues that affect you, you can always rely on me.
When you try and overcome the loneliness you feel, you can always rely on me.

When you feel down, you can always rely on me.
If and when you feel broken, you can always rely on me.
When you feel like you're in a dark place, you can always rely on me;
When you feel like you're struggling, you can always rely on me.

When your inner cries take its toll on you, you can always rely on me.
When you don't feel strong enough, you can always rely on me.
When you don't feel brave enough, you can always rely on me.
When you feel low, you can always rely on me.

When you feel lost in any way, you can always rely on me.
When you need a shoulder to cry on, you can always rely on me.
If and when you don't feel good enough, you can always rely on me.
When you feel like an outsider, you can always rely on me.

If and when you feel rejected, you can always rely on me.
When you feel like giving up, you can always rely on me.
If and when you feel unwanted, you can always rely on me.
If and when you feel worthless, you can always rely on me.

When you feel like your entering an unknown trap, you can always rely on me.
When you feel like you're in denial, you can always rely on me.
If and when you have nowhere to turn, you can always rely on me.
If and when you don't feel you have the courage to fight, you can always rely on me.

If and when you feel insecure, you can always rely on me.
If and when you feel guilt, you can always rely on me.
When you need me the most, you can always rely on me.

When you are not yourself, you can always rely on me.
When you feel alone you can always rely on me.
When you face challenging days, I will walk alongside you and you can always rely on me.
If and when you need to vent, you can always rely on me,

Fall

When you look back at your fragile past, I won't let you fall.
When you face your lifelong fears, I won't let you fall
When try and break your lifelong issues that affect you, I won't let you fall.
When you try and overcome the loneliness you feel, I won't let you fall.

When you feel down, I won't let you fall.
If and when you feel broken, I won't let you fall.
When you feel like you're in a dark place, I won't let you fall.
When you feel like you're struggling, I won't let you fall.

When your inner cries take its toll on you, I won't let you fall.
When you don't feel strong enough, I won't let you fall.
When you don't feel brave enough, I won't let you fall.
When you feel low, I won't let you fall.

When you feel lost in any way, I won't let you fall.
When you need a shoulder to cry on, I won't let you fall.
If and when you don't feel good enough, I won't let you fall.
When you feel like an outsider, I won't let you fall.

If and when you feel rejected, I won't let you fall.
When you feel like giving up, I won't let you fall.
If and when you feel unwanted, I won't let you fall.
If and when you feel worthless, I won't let you fall.

When you feel like your entering an unknown trap, I won't let you fall.
When you feel like you're in denial, I won't let you fall.
If and when you have nowhere to turn, I won't let you fall.
If and when you don't feel you have the courage to fight, I won't let you fall.

If and when you feel insecure, I won't let you fall.
If and when you feel guilt, I won't let you fall.
When you need me the most, I won't let you fall.

When you are not yourself, I won't let you fall.
When you feel alone, I won't let you fall.
When you face challenging days, I will walk alongside you, and I won't let you fall.
If and when you need to vent, I won't let you fall.

Turn You

When you look back at your fragile past, I won't turn you away.
When you face your lifelong fears, I won't turn you away.
When try and break your lifelong issues that affect you, I won't turn you away.
When you try and overcome the loneliness you feel, I won't turn you away.

When you feel down, I won't turn you away.
If and when you feel broken, I won't turn you away.
When you feel like you're in a dark place, I won't turn you away.
When you feel like you're struggling, I won't turn you away.

When your inner cries take its toll on you, I won't turn you away.
When you don't feel strong enough, I won't turn you away.
When you don't feel brave enough, I won't turn you away.
When you feel low, I won't turn you away.

When you feel lost in any way, I won't turn you away.
When you need a shoulder to cry on, I won't turn you away.
If and when you don't feel good enough, I won't turn you away.
When you feel like an outsider, I won't turn you away.

If and when you feel rejected, I won't turn you away.
When you feel like giving up, I won't turn you away.
If and when you feel unwanted, I won't turn you away.
If and when you feel worthless, I won't turn you away.

When you feel like your entering an unknown trap, I won't turn you away.
When you feel like you're in denial, I won't turn you away.
If and when you have nowhere to turn, I won't turn you away.
If and when you don't feel you have the courage to fight, I won't turn you away.

If and when you feel insecure, I won't turn you away.
If and when you feel guilt, I won't turn you away.
When you need me the most, I won't turn you away.

When you are not yourself, I won't turn you away.
When you feel alone, I won't turn you away.
When you face challenging days, I will walk alongside you, and I won't turn you away.
If and when you need to vent, I won't turn you away.

Personality

You have an amazing personality.
You have an incredible personality.
You have an excellent personality.
You have a tremendous personality.

You have a rare personality.
You have a brilliant personality.
You have an extraordinary personality.
You have a unique personality.

You have a perfect personality.
You have an awesome personality.
You have a wonderful personality.
You have a personality that shows deep within you.
You make people around you proud in so many ways.
You always make an impact on people close to and around you
You have a massive influence on people
You make such a massive difference to people and their lives.
You have a genuine personality.
You have a one in a million personality.
You have a passionate personality.
You have an outstanding personality.

You have a courageous personality.
You have a firestorm personality.
You have a mega personality.
You have a magnificent personality.

You have a carefree personality.
You have a fighting sprit personality.
You have a superb personality.
You have a kind hearted personality.
You have a golden personality.
You have a superior personality.
What if my heart burns with passion.

Always

When you look back at your fragile past, you will always have me.
When you face your lifelong fears, you will always have me.
When try and break your lifelong issues that affect you, you will always have me.
When you try and overcome the loneliness you feel, you will always have me.

When you feel down, you will always have me.
If and when you feel broken, you will always have me
When you feel like you're in a dark place, I won't turn you away.
When you feel like you're struggling, I won't turn you away.

When your inner cries take its toll on you, you will always have me.
When you don't feel strong enough, you will always have me.
When you don't feel brave enough, you will always have me.
When you feel low, you will always have me.

When you feel lost in any way, you will always have me.
When you need a shoulder to cry on, you will always have me.
If and when you don't feel good enough, you will always have me.
When you feel like an outsider, you will always have me.

If and when you feel rejected, you will always have me.
When you feel like giving up, you will always have me.
If and when you feel unwanted, you will always have me.
If and when you feel worthless, you will always have me.

When you feel like your entering an unknown trap, you will always have me.
When you feel like you're in denial, you will always have me.
If and when you have nowhere to turn, you will always have me.
If and when you don't feel you have the courage to fight, you will always have me.

If and when you feel insecure, you will always have me.
If and when you feel guilt, you will always have me.
When you need me the most, you will always have me.
When you are not yourself, you will always have me.
When you feel alone, you will always have me.
When you face challenging days, I will walk alongside you, and you will always have me.
If and when you need to vent, you will always have me.

Hear You

When you look back at your fragile past, I hear you call.

When you face your lifelong fears, I hear you call.
When you try and break your lifelong issues that affect you, I hear you call.
When you try and overcome the loneliness you feel, I hear you call,

When you feel down, I hear you call.
If and when you feel broken, I hear you call.
When you feel like you're in a dark place, I hear you call.
When you feel like you're struggling, I hear you call.

When your inner cries take its toll on you, I hear you call.
When you don't feel strong enough, I hear you call.
When you don't feel brave enough, I hear you call.
When you feel low, I hear you call.

When you feel lost in any way, I hear you call.
When you need a shoulder to cry on, I hear you call.
If and when you don't feel good enough, I hear you call.
When you feel like an outsider, I hear you call.

If and when you feel rejected, I hear you call.
When you feel like giving up, I hear you call.
If and when you feel unwanted, I hear you call.
If and when you feel worthless, I hear you call.

When you feel like your entering an unknown trap, I hear you call.
When you feel like you're in denial, I hear you call.
If and when you have nowhere to turn, I hear you call.
If and when you don't feel you have the courage to fight, I hear you call.

If and when you feel insecure, I hear you call.
If and when you feel guilt, I hear you call,
When you need me the most, I hear you call.
When you are not yourself, I hear you call.
When you feel alone, I hear you call.
When you face challenging days, I will walk alongside you, and I hear you call.
If and when you need to vent, I hear you call.

My Way

When you look back at your fragile past, always look my way.
When you face your lifelong fears, always look my way
When you try and break your lifelong issues that affect you, always look my way.
When you try and overcome the loneliness you feel, always look my way.

When you feel down, always look my way.
If and when you feel broken, always look my way.
When you feel like you're in a dark place, always look my way.
When you feel like you're struggling, always look my way.

When your inner cries take its toll on you, always look my way.
When you don't feel strong enough, always look my way.
When you don't feel brave enough, always look my way.
When you feel low, always look my way.

When you feel lost in any way, always look my way.
When you need a shoulder to cry on, always look my way.
If and when you don't feel good enough, always look my way
When you feel like an outsider, always look my way.

If and when you feel rejected, always look my way.
When you feel like giving up, always look my way.
If and when you feel unwanted, always look my way.
If and when you feel worthless, always look my way.

When you feel like your entering an unknown trap always look my way.
When you feel like you're in denial, always look my way.
If and when you have nowhere to turn, always look my way.
If and when you don't feel you have the courage to fight, always look my way.

If and when you feel insecure, always look my way.
If and when you feel guilt, always look my way,
When you need me the most, always look my way.
When you are not yourself, always look my way.
When you feel alone, always look my way.
When you face challenging days, I will walk alongside you, and always look my way.
If and when you need to vent, always look my way.

Trust

When you look back at your fragile past, know you can trust in me.
When you face your lifelong fears, know you can trust in me.
When you try and break your lifelong issues that affect you, know you can trust in me.
When you try and overcome the loneliness you feel, know you can trust in me.

When you feel down, know you trust in me.
If and when you feel broken, know you can trust in me.
When you feel like you're in a dark place, know you can trust in me
When you feel like you're struggling, know you can trust in me.

When your inner cries take its toll on you, know you can trust in me.
When you don't feel strong enough, know you can trust in me.
When you don't feel brave enough, know you can trust in me.
When you feel low, know you can trust in me.

When you feel lost in any way, know you can trust in me.
When you need a shoulder to cry on, know you can trust in me.
If and when you don't feel good enough, know you can trust in me.
When you feel like an outsider, know you can trust in me.

If and when you feel rejected, know you can trust in me.
When you feel like giving up, know you can trust in me.
If and when you feel unwanted, know you can trust in me.
If and when you feel worthless, know you can trust in me.

When you feel like your entering an unknown trap, know you can trust in me.
When you feel like you're in denial, know you can trust in me.
If and when you have nowhere to turn, know you can trust in me.
If and when you don't feel you have the courage to fight, know you can trust in me.

If and when you feel insecure, know you can trust in me.
If and when you feel guilt, know you can trust in me.
When you need me the most, know you can trust in me.
When you are not yourself, know you can trust in me.
When you feel alone, know you can trust in me.
When you face challenging days, I will walk alongside you, and know you can trust in me
If and when you need to vent, know you can trust in me

To Me

When you look back at your fragile past, know you can turn to me.
When you face your lifelong fears, know you can turn to me.
When you try and break your lifelong issues that affect you, know you can turn to me.
When you try and overcome the loneliness you feel, know you can turn to me.

When you feel down, know you turn to me.
If and when you feel broken, know you can turn to me.
When you feel like you're in a dark place, know you can turn to me
When you feel like you're struggling, know you can turn to me.

When your inner cries take its toll on you, know you can turn to me.
When you don't feel strong enough, know you can turn to me.
When you don't feel brave enough, know you can turn to me
When you feel low, know you can turn to me.

When you feel lost in any way, know you can turn to me.
When you need a shoulder to cry on, know you can turn to me.
If and when you don't feel good enough, know you can turn to me.
When you feel like an outsider, know you can turn to me.

If and when you feel rejected, know you can turn to me.
When you feel like giving up, know you can turn to me.
If and when you feel unwanted, know you can turn to me.
If and when you feel worthless, know you can turn to me.

When you feel like your entering an unknown trap, know you can turn to me.
When you feel like you're in denial, know you can turn to me.
If and when you have nowhere to turn, know you can turn to me.
If and when you don't feel you have the courage to fight, know you can turn to me,

If and when you feel insecure, know you can turn to me.
If and when you feel guilt, know you can turn to me.
When you need me the most, know you can turn to me
When you are not yourself, know you can turn to me.
When you feel alone, know you can turn to me.
When you face challenging days, I will walk alongside you, and know you can turn to me.
If and when you need to vent, know you can turn to me.

Your Side

When you look back at your fragile past, know I will never leave your side.
When you face your lifelong fears, know I will never leave your side.
When you try and break your lifelong issues that affect you, know I will never leave your side.
When you try and overcome the loneliness you feel, know I will never leave your side.

When you feel down, know I will never leave your side.
If and when you feel broken, know I will never leave your side.
When you feel like you're in a dark place, know I will never leave your side.
When you feel like you're struggling, know I will never leave your side.

When your inner cries take its toll on you, know I will never leave your side.
When you don't feel strong enough, know I will never leave your side.
When you don't feel brave enough, know I will never leave your side.
When you feel low, know I will never leave your side.

When you feel lost in any way, know I will never leave your side.
When you need a shoulder to cry on, know I will never leave your side.
If and when you don't feel good enough, know I will never leave your side.
When you feel like an outsider, know I will never leave your side.

If and when you feel rejected, know I will never leave your side.
When you feel like giving up, know I will never leave your side.
If and when you feel unwanted, know I will never leave your side.
If and when you feel worthless, know I will never leave your side.

When you feel like your entering an unknown trap, know I will never leave your side.
When you feel like you're in denial, know I will never leave your side.
If and when you have nowhere to turn, know I will never leave your side.
If and when you don't feel you have the courage to fight, know I will never leave your side.

If and when you feel insecure, know I will never leave your side.
If and when you feel guilt, know I will never leave your side.
When you need me the most, know I will never leave your side.
When you are not yourself, know I will never leave your side,
When you feel alone, know I will never leave your side.
When you face challenging days, I will walk alongside you, and know I will never leave your side.
If and when you need to vent, know I will never leave your side.

Never Let You

When you look back at your fragile past, know I will never let you down.
When you face your lifelong fears, know I will never let you down.
When you try and break your lifelong issues that affect you, know I will never let you down.
When you try and overcome the loneliness you feel, know I will never let you down.

When you feel down, know I will never let you down.
If and when you feel broken, know I will never let you down.
When you feel like you're in a dark place, know I will never let you down.
When you feel like you're struggling, know I will never let you down.

When your inner cries take its toll on you, know I will never let you down.
When you don't feel strong enough, know I will never let you down.
When you don't feel brave enough, know I will never let you down.
When you feel low, know I will never let you down.

When you feel lost in any way, know I will never let you down.
When you need a shoulder to cry on, know I will never let you down.
If and when you don't feel good enough, know I will never let you down.
When you feel like an outsider, know I will never let you down.

If and when you feel rejected, know I will never let you down.
When you feel like giving up, know I will never let you down.
If and when you feel unwanted, know I will never let you down.
If and when you feel worthless, know I will never let you down.

When you feel like you're entering an unknown trap, know I will never let you down.
When you feel like you're in denial, know I will never let you down
if and when you have nowhere to turn, know I will never let you down.
If and when you feel you don't have the courage to fight, know I will never let you down.

If and when you feel insecure, know I will never let you down.
If and when you feel guilt, know I will never let you down.
When you need me the most, know I will never let you down.
When you are not yourself, know I will never let you down.
When you feel alone, know I will never let you down.
When you face challenging days, I will walk alongside you and know I will never let you down.
If and when you need to vent know I will never let you down.

Glue You Back

When you look back at your fragile past, know I will glue you back together.
When you face your lifelong fears, know I will glue you back together.
When you try and break your lifelong issues that affect you, know I will glue you back together.
When you try and overcome the loneliness you feel, know I will glue you back together.

When you feel down, know I will glue you back together.
When you feel broken, know I will glue you back together.
When you feel like you're in a dark place, know I will glue you back together.
When you feel like you're struggling, know I will glue you back together.

When your inner cries take its toll on you, know I will glue you back together,
When you don't feel strong enough, know I will glue you back together.
When you don't feel brave enough, know I will glue you back together.
When you feel low, know I will glue you back together.

When you feel lost in any way, know I will glue you back together.
When you need a shoulder to cry on, know I will glue you back together.
If and when you don't feel good enough, know I will glue you back together.
When you feel like an outsider, know I will glue you back together.

If and when you feel rejected, know I will glue you back together.
When you feel like giving up, know I will glue you back together.
If and when you feel unwanted, know I will glue you back together.
If and when you feel worthless, know I will glue you back together.

When you feel like you're entering an unknown trap, know I will glue you back together.
When you feel like you're in denial, know I will glue you back together.
If and when you have nowhere to turn, know I will glue you back together.
If and when you feel you don't have the courage to fight, know I will glue you back together.

If and when you feel insecure, know I will glue you back together.
If and when you feel guilt, know I will glue you back together.
When you need me the most, know I will glue you back together.
When you are not yourself, know I will glue you back together.

When you feel alone, know I will glue you back together.
When face challenging days, know I will glue you back together.
If and when you need to vent, know I will glue you back together.

Hurt You

When you look back at your fragile past, know I will make sure no one hurts you.
When you face your lifelong fears, know I will make sure no one hurts you.
When you try and break your lifelong issues that affect you, know I will make sure no one hurts you.
When you try and overcome the loneliness you feel, know I will make sure no one hurts you.

When you feel down, know I will make sure no one hurts you.
When you feel broken, know I will make sure no one hurts you.
When you feel like you're in a dark place, know I will make sure no one hurts you
When you feel like you're struggling, know I will make sure no one hurts you.

When your inner cries take its toll on you, know I will make sure no one hurts you.
When you don't feel strong enough, know I will make sure no one hurts you.
When you don't feel brave enough, know I will make sure no one hurts you.
When you feel low, know I will make sure no one hurts you.

When you feel lost in any way, know I will make sure no one hurts you.
When you need a shoulder to cry on, know I will make sure no one hurts you..
If and when you don't feel good enough, know I will make sure no one hurts you.
When you feel like an outsider, know I will make sure no one hurts you.

If and when you feel rejected, know I will make sure no one hurts you.
When you feel like giving up, know I will make sure no one hurts you.
If and when you feel unwanted, know I will make sure no one hurts you.
If and when you feel worthless, know I will make sure no one hurts you.

When you feel like you're entering an unknown trap, know I will make sure no one hurts you.
When you feel like you're in denial, know I will make sure no one hurts you.
If and when you have nowhere to turn, know I will make sure no one hurts you.
If and when you feel you don't have the courage to fight, know I will make sure no one hurts you.

If and when you feel insecure, know I will make sure no one hurts you.
If and when you feel guilt, know I will make sure no one hurts you.

When you need me the most, know I will make sure no one hurts you.
When you are not yourself, know I will make sure no one hurts you.

When you feel alone, know I will make sure no one hurts you.
When face challenging days, know I will make sure no one hurts you.
If and when you need to vent, know I will make sure no one hurts you.

You Helped

You helped me figure out how to get past my traumatic past.
You helped me vanish my lifelong fears that terrorise me to no end.
You helped me find a purpose in life.
You helped me realise my potential.

You helped me turn my life around.
You helped me put my doubts to the back of my mind.
You helped me find myself.
You helped me realise I am worthy of being.

You helped me realise I am as unique as everyone else.
You helped me shape the person I am today.
You helped me by putting a smile on my face
You helped me defy the odds.

You helped me defy my expectations.
You helped me defy my pain.
You helped me defy my ongoing traumas.
You helped the true me to surface.

You helped the real me to show.
You helped me realise I am my own person.
You helped me realise I am who I wanna be.
You helped me raise my spirits.
You helped me by being a part of my life.

Blink Of An Eye

When you look back at your fragile past, know I will appear in a blink of an eye.
When you face your lifelong fears, know I will appear in a blink of an eye.
When you try and break your lifelong issues that affect you, know I will appear in a blink of an eye.
When you try and overcome the loneliness you feel, know I will appear in a blink of an eye

When you feel down, know I will appear in a blink of an eye.
When you feel broken, know I will appear in a blink of an eye.
When you feel like you're in a dark place, know I will appear in a blink of an eye.
When you feel like you're struggling, know I will appear in a blink of an eye.

When your inner cries take its toll on you, know I will appear in a blink of an eye.
When you don't feel strong enough, know I will appear in a blink of an eye.
When you don't feel brave enough, know I will appear in a blink of an eye.
When you feel low, know I will appear in a blink of an eye.

When you feel lost in any way, know I will appear in a blink of an eye.
When you need a shoulder to cry on, know I will appear in a blink of an eye.
If and when you don't feel good enough, know I will appear in a blink of an eye.
When you feel like an outsider, know I will appear in a blink of an eye.

If and when you feel rejected, know I will appear in a blink of an eye.
When you feel like giving up, know I will appear in a blink of an eye.
If and when you feel unwanted, know I will appear in a blink of an eye.
If and when you feel worthless, know I will appear in a blink of an eye.

When you feel like you're entering an unknown trap, know I will appear in a blink of an eye.
When you feel like you're in denial, know I will appear in a blink of an eye.
If and when you have nowhere to turn, know I will appear in a blink of an eye.
If and when you feel you don't have the courage to fight, know I will appear in a blink of an eye.

If and when you feel insecure, know I will appear in a blink of an eye.
If and when you feel guilt, know I will appear in a blink of an eye.
When you need me the most, know I will appear in a blink of an eye.
When you are not yourself, know I will appear in a blink of an eye.
When you feel alone, know I will appear in a blink of an eye.
When face challenging days, know I will appear in a blink of an eye.
If and when you need to vent, know I will appear in a blink of an eye

In Your Corner

When you look back at your fragile past, know I will always be in your corner.
When you face your lifelong fears, know I will always be in your corner.
When you try and break your lifelong issues that affect you, know I will always be in your corner.
When you try and overcome the loneliness you feel, know I will always be in your corner.

When you feel down, know I will always be in your corner.
When you feel broken, know I will always be in your corner.
When you feel like you're in a dark place, know I will always be in your corner.
When you feel like you're struggling, know I will always be in your corner.

When your inner cries take its toll on you, know I will always be in your corner.
When you don't feel strong enough, know I will always be in your corner.
When you don't feel brave enough, know I will always be in your corner.
When you feel low, know I will always be in your corner.

When you feel lost in any way, know I will always be in your corner.
When you need a shoulder to cry on, know I will always be in your corner.
If and when you don't feel good enough, know I will always be in your corner.
When you feel like an outsider, know I will always be in your corner.

If and when you feel rejected, know I will always be in your corner.
When you feel like giving up, know I will always be in your corner.
If and when you feel unwanted, know I will always be in your corner.
If and when you feel worthless, know I will always be in your corner.

When you feel like you're entering an unknown trap, know I will always be in your corner.
When you feel like you're in denial, know I will always be in your corner.
If and when you have nowhere to turn, know I will always be in your corner.
If and when you feel you don't have the courage to fight, know I will always be in your corner.

If and when you feel insecure, know I will always be in your corner.
If and when you feel guilt, know I will always be in your corner.
When you need me the most, know I will always be in your corner.
When you are not yourself, know I will always be in your corner.

When you feel alone, know I will always be in your corner.
When face challenging days, know I will always be in your corner.
If and when you need to vent, know I will always be in your corner.

When You Need

When you look back at your fragile past, I will know when you need me.
When you face your lifelong fears, I will know when you need me.
When you try and break your lifelong issues that affect you, I will know when you need me.
When you try and overcome the loneliness you feel, I will know when you need me.

When you feel down, I will know when you need me.
When you feel broken, I will know when you need me.
When you feel like you're in a dark place, I will know when you need me.
When you feel like you're struggling, I will know when you need me.

When your inner cries take its toll on you, I will know when you need me.
When you don't feel strong enough, I will know when you need me.
When you don't feel brave enough, I will know when you need me.
When you feel low, I will know when you need me.

When you feel lost in any way, I will know when you need me.
When you need a shoulder to cry on, I will know when you need me.
If and when you don't feel good enough, I will know when you need me.
When you feel like an outsider, I will know when you need me.

If and when you feel rejected, I will know when you need me.
When you feel like giving up, I will know when you need me.
If and when you feel unwanted, I will know when you need me.
If and when you feel worthless, I will know when you need me

When you feel like you're entering an unknown trap, I will know when you need me.
When you feel like you're in denial, I will know when you need me.
If and when you have nowhere to turn, I will know when you need me.
If and when you feel you don't have the courage to fight, I will know when you need me.

If and when you feel insecure, I will know when you need me.
If and when you feel guilt, I will know when you need me.
When you need me the most, I will know when you need me.
When you are not yourself, I will know when you need me.

When you feel alone, I will know when you need me.
When face challenging days, I will know when you need me.
If and when you need to vent, I will know when you need me.

Index

A Star	**79**
Admire	**84**
Against	**31**
Always	**135**
An Act	**40**
Angel Eyez	**44**
Apart	**124**
Approach	**118**
Around You	**56**
B F	**105**
Backstab	**64**
Believe In	**27**
Betray	**68**
Blame Game	**12**
Blink Of A Light	**13**
Blink Of An Eye	**145**
Brave	**36**
Break Through	**71**
Bring You Down	**58**
Care	**21**
Cave In	**20**
Cling	**85**
Close By	**50**
Connection	**60**
Count	**128**
Crossroads	**37**
Crumble	**29**
Defeat	**57**
Doubt	**72**
Drag Down	**34**
Dreams	**52**
Drown	**87**
Eliminate	**89**
Errors	**98**
Every Inch	**33**
Extra Mile	**100**
Fake	**38**
Fall	**132**

Fall Out	**113**
Family Loyalty	**52**
Feel	**73**
For Me	**110**
Free	**16**
Glue You Back	**142**
Heal	**24**
Hear You	**136**
Hero	**106**
Hit A Brick Wall	**70**
Hold	**65**
Host	**81**
Human Being	**108**
Hurt You	**143**
I Give	**10**
If	**75**
Illusion	**55**
Imperfections	**111**
In A Flash	**26**
In The Flesh	**11**
In Your Corner	**146**
Individuality	**123**
Inseparable	**48**
Inspiration	**107**
Intentions	**101**
Interest	**103**
Intoxicated	**42**
Keep Close	**32**
Knock Down	**17**
Lead Astray	**54**
Lean On	**126**
Let My Voice	**91**
Light	**122**
Living Proof	**120**
Look	**19**
Look Out	**22**
Loyal	**23**
Loyalty	**18**
My Back	**115**
My Hand	**109**
My Way	**137**
Never	**99**

Never Change	76
Never Let	28
Never Let You	141
Never Question	60
Over You	93
Perfect	92
Personality	134
Pick Myself	41
Power	25
Protector	14
Reach Out	125
Rely	131
Reservations	35
Rise Above It	25
Rock	130
Role Model.	114
Screw	88
Shield Me	62
Smile	30
So Caught Up	59
Spiral	47
Stand Tall	39
Stick By	51
Storm	63
Take Advantage	66
Teardrop	46
Thank You	112
The Absolute World	74
The Best	90
The Warrior	86
The Worst	95
To Me	139
Trust	138
Turn You	133
Under Your Wing	117
Underground	61
Unlock	45
Untangle	53
Up To Me	80
Up To You	78
Vent	127
Vision	47

Vision Impairment	**119**
Walk Away	**15**
Walk On Fire	**97**
When	**33**
When You Need	**147**
Wish	**77**
Worst Enemy	**49**
You Have	**32**
You Helped	**144**
Your Back	**129**
Your Shell	**82**
Your Side	**140**
Yourself	**43**

If you liked reading this book then you will like the following books of fictional work.

MA Publisher Catalogue

ISBN/Titles /Image/Author	Descriptions
978-1-910499-02-3 (eBook) & 978-1-910499-00-9 (Paperback) Father to child  By Mayar Akash	This EBook version Father to Child is a collection of inspirational poems and musings that follow the author's life from his own childhood up to when he had children of his own, and wishes to pass some of wisdom to them.
978-1-910499-16-0 River of Life  By Mayar Akash	This journey in the river of life, a metaphor for living, a contrast between the British life and the Bangladeshi lives' in both parts of the world. Reflect on the integrational change acquired and adopted as a result of living in UK.
978-1-910499-14-6 The Halloweeen Poem  By Zainab Khan	This short poetry book written by Zainab who was an 8-year-old. She writes about her experience of Halloween in poetry form, especially as a young Bangladeshi Muslim growing up and integrating into the British society and how these customs have become her school and daily life.

978-1-910499-36-8 Delirious  By Liam Newton	Music is powerful enough to change people's views on aspects of the society they live in or the world around them. It magnifies the actual feelings the artist feels and shares with others their experience. In this book the writer gives the reader snapshot insight of his life in the form of lyrics. Music keeps him going and hope it keeps you going too
978-1-910499-39-9 Eyewithin 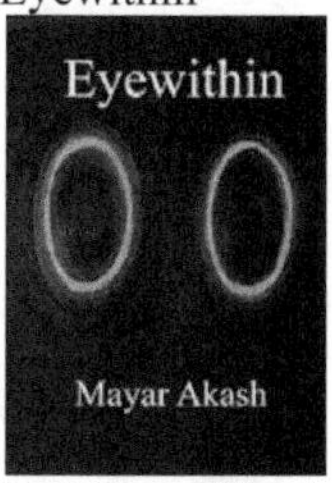 By Mayar Akash	This is the 3rd book of Mayar Akash. The book catalogues the lost paintings by himself.
978-1-910499-37-5 My Dream World  By Rashma Mehta	This is the first of Rashma's book filled with her imaginary world of experiences and perception.

29/3/2019 (Brexit day - Postponed)

CPSIA information can be obtained
at www.ICGtesting.com
Printed in the USA
BVHW040941200519
548789BV00030B/2844/P

9 781910 499412